The Scramble for Europe

For Charlie and Anne

The Scramble for Europe

Young Africa on its Way to the Old Continent

Stephen Smith

polity

First published in French as *La ruée vers l'Europe* © Éditions Grasset & Fasquelle, 2018

This English edition © Polity Press, 2019

Polity Press
65 Bridge Street
Cambridge CB2 1UR, UK

Polity Press
101 Station Landing
Suite 300
Medford, MA 02155, USA

ISBN-13: 978-1-5095-3456-2
ISBN-13: 978-1-5095-3457-9 (pb)

A catalogue record for this book is available from the British Library.

Library of Congress Cataloging-in-Publication Data
Names: Smith, Stephen, 1956- author.
Title: The scramble for Europe : young Africa on its way to the old continent
  / Stephen Smith.
Description: Medford, MA : Polity, 2019. | Includes bibliographical
  references and index.
Identifiers: LCCN 2018046811 (print) | LCCN 2018055560 (ebook) | ISBN
  9781509534586 (Epub) | ISBN 9781509534562 (hardback) | ISBN 9781509534579
  (pbk.)
Subjects: LCSH: Human geography--Africa, Sub-Saharan. | Human
  geography--Europe. | Africans--Migration. | Africans--Europe. |
  Immigrants--Europe. | Africa, Sub-Saharan--Emigration and immigration. |
  Europe--Emigration and immigration.
Classification: LCC GF701 (ebook) | LCC GF701 .S62 2019 (print) | DDC
  304.8/406--dc23
LC record available at https://lccn.loc.gov/2018046811

Typeset in 10.75 on 14 pt Janson Text by
Servis Filmsetting Ltd, Stockport, Cheshire
Printed and bound in Great Britain by TJ International Limited

The publisher has used its best endeavours to ensure that the URLs for external websites referred to in this book are correct and active at the time of going to press. However, the publisher has no responsibility for the websites and can make no guarantee that a site will remain live or that the content is or will remain appropriate.

Every effort has been made to trace all copyright holders, but if any have been overlooked the publisher will be pleased to include any necessary credits in any subsequent reprint or edition.

For further information on Polity, visit our website:
politybooks.com

Contents

Acknowledgements

This book is a labour of friendship. It would not exist without the generous help of those who have seen me through first the process of writing the French original and then the similarly daunting task of producing a *belle infidèle* in English – an entirely updated and reworked version, purged of (almost) all of my beloved Gallicisms and the scoriae of half-baked thought. In France, Olivier Nora, my publisher at the helm of Grasset, and Ronald Blunden, the head of communications for the Hachette Group (who even made 'detours' to my home in North Carolina), have been inexhaustible sources of excellent counsel. In the United States, T. R. Goldman and Sam Fury Childs Daly – a fellow journalist and a fellow Africanist at Duke – have done yeoman's service to standardize my idiosyncratic English (I grew up speaking German with my mother and have lived outside the US, in Europe and Africa, for forty-five years). In England, Mark Huband – with whom I wrote joint dispatches out of Monrovia in the early 1990s, when the Liberian capital was besieged by Charles Taylor – also offered more than one welcome suggestion. And, finally, Jeremy Harding, a contributing editor of *The London*

Review of Books who lives in southwestern France, went through the final draft and laid it all to rest. I owe him more than any words of thanks could convey. In the end, of course, I am solely responsible for the content of this book. Alas, it is less perfect than the support I received, including from my new friends in the making at Polity Books, John Thompson and the entire team.

Further, I want to acknowledge my debt to Richard Cincotta, the director of demographic studies at the Stimson Center in Washington DC, to whom I owe my discovery of the 'human geography' of Africa. With kindness and patience, he introduced me to the complexities of his world.

My thanks also go to Charles Piot and Achille Mbembé. Together, we organized two international migration conferences at Duke University, which gathered scholars from across Africa, Europe and North America. This book owes a great deal to their numerous insights.

Last but not least, I will be forever grateful to all the African migrants – in Africa, Europe and the United States – for their trust in sharing their life stories with me. They sent me on the journey that eventually led to this book.

Introduction: A View from the Top of the Population Pyramid

At the Summer Olympic Games in London in 2012, the oldest competitor was a Japanese equestrian, Hiroshi Hoketsu. At seventy-one, he had qualified for the games for the third time. The youngest athlete, Adzo Kpossi, a thirteen-year-old swimmer from Togo, was competing in the 50-metre freestyle. Neither won a medal, but the two athletes did represent opposite ends of the global demographic spectrum. Hoketsu came from a state that since the 1970s has had the oldest population in the world. Kpossi came from a small country in sub-Saharan Africa, a region with the largest concentration of young people anywhere on the planet. That a Togolese girl and a Japanese man represented the bottom and top of the Olympic age pyramid was not entirely accidental, any more than the fact that London, just a few years later, would become the first European capital to elect a Muslim as its mayor, and a first-generation Briton at that. The May 2016 election of Sadiq Khan, born on British soil to parents who had arrived from Pakistan in 1970, was, for some, emblematic of London's cosmopolitan character. For others, it was a confirmation of their worst fears: they were becoming strangers in their own land. The

polarized readings reflect London's radically changed demographics. In the 1950s, the British capital had roughly the same
number of inhabitants as today, but an overwhelming majority of
Londoners had parents as well as grandparents who were British.
Now, more than half of the city's inhabitants are either first or
second-generation immigrants (Collier 2013: 129).

Ordinarily, the subject of human geography, or 'demography'
as it's more often called, tends to make one's eyes glaze over.
Beyond the complicated statistics and age-related cohorts, there
is also a question of scale. Demographic changes take place too
slowly to be noticed in the day-to-day, until that moment of
coalescence when they are suddenly blindingly obvious. 'It happened, as things do, imperceptibly, in many ways at once', James
Baldwin wrote in his 1962 'Letter From a Region in my Mind',
referring to his own sudden awakening about the pervasiveness of
American racism. Two years after Baldwin's essay, Peter Griffith,
the Conservative candidate in British parliamentary elections in
Smethwick, a coal and steel town near Birmingham in the West
Midlands, ran on the slogan 'If you want a nigger for a neighbour,
vote Liberal or Labour.' Nationally, after thirteen years in opposition, Labour coasted to victory with a comfortable margin. But
in Smethwick, Griffith defeated the Labour MP Patrick Gordon
Walker, even though the latter had been widely expected to
become the party's next foreign secretary. At the time, Smethwick
was thought to be an anomaly, a short-lived racist flare-up. But
after the UK's stunning June 2016 vote to exit the European
Union, Smethwick suddenly stood out like a long-forgotten
warning sign. Polish migrants were the referendum's targets of
choice: more than a million had moved to Great Britain in the
five years following Poland's entry into the EU in 2004. Racism,
it turns out, is only one form of rejection among many. And
Smethwick, now a town where 'white Britons' account for only
38 per cent of the population, supported Brexit by a two-thirds
margin.[1] Among the reasons given by first and second-generation
immigrants to explain the vote were, in order of importance:

the preference given to EU citizens rather than members of the Commonwealth to settle in the UK; local shopkeepers' refusal to accept Polish businesses as competitors; and opposition to the neoliberal policies of the European Union.

What was it that had happened in Great Britain in half a century, or roughly an adult life span? When V. S. Naipaul, the grandchild of an immigrant Indian couple in Trinidad and Tobago, arrived in London in 1950 – then the most important capital of any colonial power – Great Britain had about 25,000 non-white immigrants (French 2008: 66). Naipaul was eighteen years old. Boarding his plane in Port of Spain, he had left his family without looking back, his eyes fixed firmly on his shadow in front of him, 'a dancing dwarf on the tarmac'. When he landed, he swore that he would 'show these people that I can beat them at their own language' (Naipaul 1983: 46, 77), a goal he achieved in 2001 when he was awarded the Nobel Prize for literature. Naipaul had become both a modern Homer and a wily Odysseus, turning deracination into a wilful opportunity for self-reinvention.

By 2001, nearly 8 per cent of the UK's population were immigrants, some 4.6 million people, a figure that had risen to 13.6 per cent by 2015, according to Britain's Office for National Statistics. A lot or a little? Everyone has an opinion, and it is largely a matter for the British to determine the answer, just as the Japanese will decide whether the inhabitants of their country who were born elsewhere – about 1.5 per cent – are too many or too few. And it's up to Americans to determine whether the US remains a country welcoming 'your tired, your poor, your huddled masses yearning to breathe free, the wretched refuse of your teeming shores', in the words of Emma Lazarus, engraved on a bronze plaque inside the Statue of Liberty. Researching and writing this book, I have made no a priori assumptions in favour of homogeneity or diversity as ideals, least of all as moral impera-tives. I don't level criticism at the Japanese for their apparent desire to remain 'among themselves' (whatever this means), or applaud the American call to embrace 'diversity' (whatever that means, assuming it is still the case). Nor do I question whether the African migrants who feature in this book are fleeing violence and lawlessness, poverty or lack of opportunity, for a better life. Nor do I insist on a distinction between legal and unauthorized migration, or between economic migrants and people seeking asylum under the terms of the 1951 Convention on the Status of Refugees.[2] That is the business of signatory states. Not that I think these are trivial issues: on the contrary, they often define a migrant's destiny, and always frame a discussion that I believe to be essential. My purpose, however, is not to stoke further controversy in debates around migration, but to provide a factual basis on which others can come to an informed view. In particular, I endeavour to assess Africa's importance as a reservoir of migrants, and as far as possible to predict both the magnitude and timing of this human flow from Africa to Europe. Under certain conditions, which I will lay out in detail, more than 100 million Africans are likely to cross the Mediterranean Sea over the next two generations. As a result, like many European families who had an 'American uncle' in the first half of the twentieth century, many African families will have a nephew or a niece in Europe in the second half of the twenty-first century.

Naipaul and a cohort of ambitious migrants, including the novelists George Lamming and Sam Selvon, arrived in the UK from the Caribbean in the 1950s neither as 'invading foreigners' nor as 'innocent victims'. They came as pioneers relying on strength of character in order to build a future that had eluded them at home. They left the land where they had been born to settle in a country that had already been fully formed by a long history of constant adaptation. As we will see, both Naipaul's new homeland and the 'dwarf' from Trinidad and Tobago were transformed in what can be described either as a postcolonial encounter in the shadow of British imperialism or a migratory encounter in the context of accelerated globalization. The two perspectives are complementary. I draw on both in the course of this book.

Three key scenes define cross-border migration. The first is the moment of abandonment, with departing people fuelled by frustration and ambition, oppression and opportunism: most often, the mix is neither pure nor simple to analyse. The second scene – the trial – transforms these fugitives into heroes, either tragic or triumphant, as they endure the various obstacles that bar them from reaching the promised land. Finally, the third scene – 'incorporation', the last stage in any rite of passage – is defined by a wager on the part of immigrants as well as their future fellow citizens that they will find common ground to inhabit together. That is to say that the act of migration is not simply realized upon arrival in a new land; its success or failure can be determined only after a period of time, sometimes only by the second or even third generation. The act of immigration engages the migrant and their descendants as much as it engages the country that eventually becomes, more or less, their home.

Africa: The Mexico of Europe

This book explores the human geography of Africa, in particular sub-Saharan Africa. It offers a living tableau of Europe's neighbouring continent and reaches a conclusion that may well be controversial: Young Africa will rush towards the Old Continent in an inversion of Europe's 'Scramble for Africa' at the end of the nineteenth century. Only this time, the initiative comes from the people, the *demos*, moving en masse to redraw the world map. European imperialism, by contrast, was driven by a small, influential minority who inspired a new imperial imaginary fostered by a revolution in communications – 'high-speed rotary presses, automatic paper folders, linotype machines, news photography, railroads, and telephones' (Berenson 2011: 9–10). The poor and disenfranchised European masses read the 'penny papers' but left in droves for the Americas, and not for Africa. Indeed, from a demographic perspective, European colonialism in Africa was a failure, even if you include its settler colonies – which, in fact, were few and far between. In 1930, the number of European citizens from the major colonial powers – Great Britain, France, Portugal and Belgium – living in Africa was fewer than 2 million, about 2 per cent of their total population and less than 1 per cent of Africa's population at the time (Ferenzci 1938: 230). On the other hand, as we will see, the current 'repopulation of the Earth by new cycles of migratory circulation', as the Cameroonian political theorist Achille Mbembé puts it (2016: 8), is driven by popular demand.

In 1885, at the conclusion of the Conference of Berlin, which established the rules for the colonial partition of sub-Saharan Africa, Europe's scientific prowess, industrialization and modern armies made it the most developed continent in the world. It counted some 275 million inhabitants, not including Russia. Africa, with six and a half times the surface area, had only 100 million inhabitants, and was the least developed continent in the world. Relatively isolated by the Sahara Desert (a land mass as vast as the continental United States), uncooperative trade winds and the scourge of malaria – 'the most formidable guardian of Africa's secrets', according to the Arab explorer Ibn Battuta – Africa's interior had barely been mapped. At a time when the aspiration 'to reign on earth' was taken literally, when Christianity and the Enlightenment cult of progress were ardently proselytized, when other continents were already conquered and previously closed countries like Japan had been forcibly opened to 'free trade', it would have taken a minor miracle for Africa to escape European domination.

It would be equally astonishing if Europe were not acutely concerned with the next massive South-North migration rippling across the globe from the less developed regions of the world. Between 1960 and 2000, South-to-North flows rapidly accelerated, with the total number of migrants tripling from 20 to 60 million (Collier 2013: 50).[3] Except for the Maghreb, whose inhabitants left almost exclusively for France, Africa has so far played only a minor role in these migratory waves, which emanated mostly from Asia and South America. Sub-Saharan Africa was still too poor and marginalized to play a part. And it is still relatively

poor: in 1960, a little more than half its population lived in absolute poverty; today that figure is a little less than half, according to
the World Bank. Yet at the same time, the population south of the
Sahara has more than quadrupled, jumping to more than 1 billion
in 2015 from some 230 million in 1960. It is also more and more
in step with the rest of the world, to which it is now connected
by satellite television stations, mobile telephones and broadband
technology. Half of the continent's population now has access
to 4G telephony or the internet, through fibre-optic submarine
cables enabling video streaming and the downloading of vast
quantities of other data. And, finally, emerging from this sea of
poverty is a real middle class. Some 150 million African consumers now have a disposable income equal to anywhere from 5 to
20 US dollars per day. Not far behind are another 200 million
people with a *per diem* income of 2 to 5 dollars. In short, a growing number of Africans are in the global information loop and can
muster the resources to seek their fortune elsewhere.

The situation is reminiscent of Mexico in the 1970s. Before
then, only a tiny fraction of the population could scrape together
the wherewithal to cross the Rio Grande and settle in the United
States. But as their country crossed a threshold into relative
prosperity, more and more Mexicans decided to depart. Between
1975 and 2010, 10 million Mexicans migrated to America both
legally and illegally. In all, including their children born in the
United States, Mexican-Americans now form a community of
some 30 million people, about 10 per cent of the US population.
If Africans followed that example between now and 2050, the
Afro-optimistic leitmotiv of 'Africa Rising' would, quite literally,
become a reality (cf. Mahajan 2008; Radelet 2010). At the end of
a sustained African migratory wave, Europe's population would
include some 150 to 200 million African-Europeans – counting
immigrants and their children – compared with just 9 million
today. In a little more than thirty years, between one-fifth and
one-quarter of the population in Europe would be of African
descent (Millman 2015).[4]

An absurd fantasy? A sensationalist prediction? History is never written ahead of time – past events can be grossly misleading, or misinterpreted, while different demographic projections as well as the magnitude and duration of future migratory patterns can vary significantly. Moreover, Europe may not be the quasi-exclusive destination for Africans that America was for Mexicans. Comparisons are also less apt because Africa is not a single country neighbouring Europe, and the Mediterranean is a far more redoubtable body of water to cross than the Rio Grande. On the other hand, in 1975, the population of America was three and a half times Mexico's then 60 million inhabitants, while today it is still two and a half times larger, although the Mexican population has doubled. Even if we take into account *all* of Latin America, with its 600 million or so inhabitants, the migratory pressures on the United States are much weaker than those facing Europe. Today, the European Union (including the United Kingdom) has some 510 million inhabitants, while there are 1.3 billion people in neighbouring Africa. In thirty-five years, that asymmetry will have grown enormously – there will be an estimated 450 million Europeans and some 2.5 billion Africans. As the population of Europe continues to age, Africa's demographic will continue to trend in the opposite direction. By 2050, two-thirds of Africans will be less than thirty years old. Put another way, for every European in their fifties, there will be three Africans, two of whom will be in the prime of life.

I can imagine how Europeans might quake at the thought. Their fears are by no means groundless, as I try to show towards the end of this book. But I was impelled to write it not as a demographer – I am not – or an alarmist Eurocentric – I am not – but as someone who has spent most of his working life engaged with sub-Saharan Africa, reporting its news as a journalist, and later researching its less eye-catching realities as an academic. I do not lie awake at night trembling at the prospect of an 'Africanization' of Europe (which, in any event, has been underway since the 1920s). Rather the reverse: the very real possibility of an exodus from Africa haunts me because I find it hard to accept that the continent could become an abandoned hulk in the eyes of its teeming youth – so demoralized by their prospects on the one hand, so robust and dogged on the other – that ever larger numbers would head for the Mediterranean. That would be a bitter admission of defeat. Yet I am forced to acknowledge that sub-Saharan Africa's foreseeable future, over the next two or three generations, is overshadowed by the monolithic nature of its demography and the pressure that seems likely to exert in favour of migration.

A 'Stress Test' Between Generations

The youthfulness of sub-Saharan Africa – a lasting consequence of the unprecedented demographic growth that began in the years between the two world wars – is crucial. Right now, more than four out of ten people on the African continent are less than fifteen years old[5] – a fundamental fact whose implications are difficult to grasp. The consequences arising from an age pyramid, 40 per cent of which comprises children or young adolescents, are as manifold and unforeseeable as it is challenging for a European or American to imagine life on just one or two dollars a day – a frequent reference in the development literature. In France, a country with a relatively high birth rate compared to the rest of Europe, the proportion of the population below the age of fourteen is still less than 20 per cent, half the rate of Africa. In sub-Saharan Africa, four out of every ten inhabitants were not yet born when the World Trade Center was destroyed in 2001; eight out of ten inhabitants were not born when the Berlin Wall fell in 1989. Because the average age is so low, the continent's collective experience is foreshortened by the sheer size of its demographic youth bubble. With the voting age at eighteen or older in fifty-three of fifty-four African countries, the continent's collective future will scarcely be determined by the majority of its citizens: at any moment you choose to look at it, half the continent's population is too young to vote. And by the time this half of the population accedes to voting age, another half of the population without the right to vote has been born. The upshot is that democracy appears more an age-based privilege than a majoritarian right.

This rapid generational turnover in sub-Saharan Africa has repercussions for every aspect of society: from questions of war and peace to those of democratization, the economy and the labour market, education and public health. If two-thirds of the world's HIV-positive people live in sub-Saharan Africa, along with two-thirds of the world's child soldiers, it's not because HIV/AIDS is an 'African malady' or that war on the continent is 'endemic'. The explanation, rather, is that a high proportion of youth means a larger number of people who are more sexually active and less cautious, especially when they've already dodged death in a thousand other ways. And in the absence of more peaceful alternatives, some swell the ranks of armed movements as foot soldiers. They're fighting what was known in the European Middle Ages as *guerre guerroyante* – war for war's sake or war as a way of life.

A population pyramid with a broad base – the term 'youth bulge'[6] is often employed – also erodes the principle of seniority, one of the bedrock social and cultural rules of sub-Saharan Africa. Seniority involves the prestige, privilege and authority normally awarded, *ipso facto*, to the elderly – especially to men – who have lived long enough to have a large, extended family or clan; who rise to positions of power and accumulate after many years a particular aggregation of knowledge that we refer to as 'wisdom'. 'In Africa', according to Amadou Hampâté Bâ's oft-cited phrase, 'when an old person dies, it is a library that burns'. But the elderly are also gerontocrats, hoarding opportunities at the expense of young men and women, before ceding their place to the next generation. The tension in contemporary Africa between the old and the young is acute. The old are the gatekeepers of a supposedly stable but actually moribund world held in place by flagrant injustices. The young yearn for equality and – propelled by constant disappointment and mounting frustration – threaten to bring the old order down on the heads of their elders.

For sub-Saharan Africa's two majority groups with minority rights – young people and women – the social contract is laced with inequities. And they are no longer patiently waiting their turn for more power and prosperity. Either by force of arms or the ballot box, new forms of digital knowledge or new articles of religious faith, from Pentecostal to Islamic, millenarian to Islamist, these 'social cadets' are struggling for emancipation. If they succeed, they will dislodge their elders. If they fail, they will look elsewhere to graduate to adulthood. Transcontinental migration is their best and most likely option. Whatever happens, Africa's 'moral reproduction' is already compromised by a numerical mismatch. Even assuming everyone over the age of sixty were automatically wise, the 'old sages' make up only 5 per cent of the population, a number that is simply not big enough for norms and values to be transmitted to the continent's young population. In the sub-Saharan slums, nine out of every ten inhabitants are less than thirty years old; they have only their peers as mentors in a life that can aspire to no more than simply 'getting by'. Like capillaries of globalization, these young people are plugged into the outside world by all the modern technology that is foreign to their elders. Their actions exacerbate what Jean-François Bayart has labelled the 'historic extraversion' of their continent (2010: 133). They are alienated in their own land.

The numerical mismatch between young and old in sub-Saharan Africa is the main driver of a massive uprooting. Ancestral cultures are barely celebrated now except at festivals subsidized by international donors who otherwise are doing everything in their power to pulverize centuries of indigenous African tradition and globalize the continent. As a result, Africans escape through the satellite dish or the internet; their 'elsewhere' begins long before they actually set out for it: a nearby town, a national or regional capital in a better-off neighbouring country, and eventually Europe, America, China . . . In Togo, which has almost 8 million inhabitants, one adult in three entered the US government lottery for a residence permit – even though the 'visa lottery' contains just 55,000 green cards for the entire world, offered to 'diversity candidates' from countries with low immigration rates to the United States.[7] In neighbouring Ghana, 6 per cent of the population – 1.7 million people out of 28 million – applied for the programme in 2015 alone, and that proportion was even surpassed in Liberia (8 per cent), Sierra Leone (8 per cent) and the Republic of Congo (10 per cent).[8] Across the whole continent, according to a 2016 Gallup Institute survey, 42 per cent of all Africans aged fifteen to twenty-four, and 32 per cent of university graduates, said they wanted to emigrate.[9] Surveys conducted in 2017 by the US-based Pew Research Center in four of the top ten countries of origin of sub-Saharan migrants now living in Europe and the United States – Nigeria, Senegal, Ghana and Kenya – have corroborated these findings. At least four in ten respondents in each country declared their intention to migrate, if they had the means and the opportunity, including a staggering three-quarters of those surveyed in Ghana (75 per cent) and Nigeria (74 per cent), Africa's most populous nation with an estimated 190 million inhabitants.[10]

In 1997, the then *Washington Post* Africa correspondent, Keith Richburg, in his book *Out of America: A Black Man Confronts Africa*, raised a hue and cry when he congratulated himself on the deportation of his African ancestors to the New World, where, despite discrimination and other hardships, they managed to succeed. To greater consternation, he wondered how quickly an African slave ship docked in a West African port would fill up with volunteers for a voyage to America. Twenty years later, Africans are routinely piling into frail skiffs at their own risk to cross the Mediterranean.

Africa Has Not Yet Taken Off

2015 was a record year for migration to Europe, occasioned by wars in Syria, Iraq and Afghanistan. Frontex, the European

Border and Coast Guard Agency, recorded that 1.256 million people immigrated to Europe that year: a million reached the continent via the Mediterranean. According to Frontex, 200,000 came from Africa; the International Organization for Migration put the figure at twice that number (IOM 2018: 38, 407). Except for Somalis and South Sudanese, who are fleeing broken states, and Eritreans escaping a ruthless dictatorship, the lives of these departing Africans are rarely in imminent danger or subject to systematic repression or famine. More often they are simply looking for a better life for themselves and their children – 'simply' not implying here that their decision is a free choice, given their frequently punishing circumstances. The number of Africans attempting to cross the Mediterranean to Europe has remained more or less constant both before and since this latest 'migrant crisis'. In 2016, while their total number fell to one-third the level the year before – from 1 million to about 360,000 – the number of Africans arriving via the main maritime route, most of them from Libya, grew by 20 per cent to some 180,000 persons.[11] That is in line with the level of documented arrivals from all routes every year over the last decade. Since 2007, 2 million Africans have arrived in Europe, or roughly 200,000 per year. According to the IOM, these 2 million have added to a 'stock' of African migrants in Europe, estimated at 9 million in 2016. That number was less than 900,000 in 1960, the year many African nations became independent. By 1997 it had risen to just 3 million, two-thirds of whom were from Morocco, Algeria and Tunisia.

Since the 1990s, three major trends have characterized migration from Africa to Europe. First, the proportion of migrants from the Maghreb has continued to decline as North African countries have completed their demographic transition from big families with short life expectancies to smaller families with longer life expectancies. At the same time, emigration from countries south of the Sahara has increased in proportion to their growing population: there are now roughly 1 billion people in sub-Saharan Africa compared with about 300 million in North Africa. In addition, the percentage of Africans migrating *within* their continent, to another African country more prosperous than their own, has dropped by comparison with the numbers leaving the continent: between 1990 and 2013, there was a threefold increase of Africans moving within Africa, while those leaving altogether jumped by a factor of six (IMF 2016: 2). Finally, African migratory patterns have become globalized, extending well beyond the four major colonial powers – France, Great Britain, Portugal and Belgium – and now encompassing the whole of Europe as well as the United States, Canada, even China and the countries of the Arab peninsula.

According to a UN study published in 2000, the European Union will need to welcome almost 50 million immigrants by 2050, about 1 million a year, just to keep its current population constant (United Nations Population Division 2000). The study assumes that the population will continue to age, and that the ratio of working-age adults to dependants – children and the retired elderly – will drop from 4.3 to 2.2. If the goal is to stabilize the *working* population in the EU – that is, people between the ages of fifteen and sixty-four – then roughly 80 million immigrants will be needed by 2050, the equivalent of 1.6 million a year (this, of course, doesn't factor in the proportion of the European workforce that artificial intelligence will have replaced by then). Even after the dramatic influx in 2015, however, Europe is not prepared for numbers of this magnitude. Immigration remains a political minefield, both on 'upstream' issues like entry requirements and border controls and 'downstream' concerns involving numerous, sometimes conflicting, models of social integration. In Poland, to take one example of a country that propounds the concept of 'ethnic homogeneity',[12] the threshold of tolerance was crossed long ago and a 'Fortress Europe' mentality is seen as the *sine qua non* for survival. For others, notably Germany, 'welcoming' people in need is a categorical imperative, and any attempt to question the unqualified acceptance of migrants is viewed as *Fremdenfeindlichkeit* or xenophobia.[13] Supporters of a 'dispassionate' debate point out that with the ageing of Europe's own population, the only way to maintain its present standard of living is to stock the continent's offices and factories with brains and brawn from elsewhere (but, again, we run up against the possibility that the surge in artificial intelligence is already providing for this shortage). If their viewpoint appears more rational, it is only because it eschews the Manichean view of all or nothing – 'our borders are either open or closed'. But it brings its own set of problems with it. First, family reunification. Given the size of the average African family, the ratio of working-age adults to dependants in Europe will not – as intended – improve but deteriorate: many more younger children in Europe will require day care, health care and education. Then there is a sort of biopolitical 'Taylorism', the theory of scientific management that chops up workers into discrete parts – bodies for the factory, brains for the office – a theory that works to the advantage of the employer. Only in this case we are talking about men and women who must find their place in their host country, not just in the workforce. Who pays for the extra costs – the language courses, the housing subsidies, the many expenses that arise as the immigrant moves through the stages of arrival and absorption? Neither the Left nor the Right has any difficulty landing these 'negative externalities' on the tax payer. For the purpose of greater equity, a far more coherent strategy would be to pass the costs on to employers in the form of a Pigovian tax, named after the British economist Arthur Cecil Pigou (1877–1957), who first came up with the idea of a corrective tax to recoup the social costs of production.

'Migration has been politicized before it has been analysed', according to Paul Collier, the co-director of the Centre for the Study of African Economies at Oxford and the author of *Exodus: How Migration is Changing Our World* (2013: 246). He laments the fact that the immigration debate poses a choice between Scylla and Charybdis – in this case either a closed-door or an open-door immigration policy – instead of seeking a navigable passageway between the two by adopting an actual immigration *policy*. If an influx of foreigners is the nightmare scenario that some have imagined, how have countries like America and Australia been able to create such prosperity? On the other hand, if immigration is the only lifeline for an ageing society, how has Japan survived with no external inputs? Collier believes that the unconditional freedom to settle wherever one wants is 'the stuff of teenage dreams': taken to its logical extension, it would mean that the whole world would move to the country offering the best opportunities, the greatest wealth, and the best prospects for the future. According to Collier (2013: 16), the blind spot of such a utopia is the possibility that the wealthy would likewise decide to settle 'freely' in some parts of the Third World. And then, of course, we would hear the cry of 'colonialism has returned!'

The Kingdom of Lies

Until the beginning of the twenty-first century, Europe paid little, if any, attention to its demographic decline and the challenges of a rapidly ageing population, deliberately ignoring what was all too obvious. The inversion of the age pyramid in Italy, Germany, Spain and Greece – where for the first time in history the number of people over the age of sixty surpassed those under the age of twenty – attracted the attention of just a handful of demographers already monitoring the situation.[14] In March 2000, when the heads of state and governments of the European Union gathered in Lisbon to decide their strategy for the coming decade, neither the EU's changing demography nor its incipient immigration tensions figured on the agenda. That they failed to address this rapidly developing issue is all the more astonishing given that Brussels is home to a greater percentage of 'third-country' immigrants than almost any other city in Europe. From 2000 onwards, half of the children born in Brussels had immigrant parents, and Muslims represented one out of four inhabitants under the age of twenty-five (Laqueur 2007: 14–15). Politicians, of course, were not the only ones with their heads in the sand. Journalists, columnists and academics, the people who help shape public debate, ceded discussion of the social discontent around immigration to the extreme right and nascent populist movements. Working in their own bubbles, they appeared blithely unaware of the growing social media storm gathering under their noses. Americans, it seemed, could be quicker than many Europeans to take up the challenge. In 2005 Robert J. Samuelson in the *Washington Post* announced 'The End of Europe', a continent he said would soon be short on both children and economic growth. Two years later, Walter Laqueur's book *The Last Days of Europe: Epitaph for an Old Continent* appeared. Unfortunately, like Bruce Bawer in 2006, Laqueur muddied the debate by linking Europe's demographic decline specifically to the challenge that Islamic fundamentalism posed to the Old Continent. In his eyes, Europe was guilty of 'tolerating intolerance' (Bawer 2002, 2006).

In all this, the human geography of Africa has not received the attention it deserves. Beyond passing acknowledgements of historically unprecedented demographic growth, the subject has rarely aroused a lot of curiosity or inspired much research. The bibliography provided to doctoral students specializing in Africa at SAIS, the School of Advanced International Studies at Johns Hopkins University, lists 212 works on the African economy, sixty-three dealing with questions of ethnicity, thirty-four on African religions – but only two titles about African demography.[15] Certainly, since the beginning of the 1990s, and the enlistment of a large number of child soldiers in a decade marked by numerous wars, 'youth' in Africa has become an obligatory section in any literature about the continent put out by the United Nations, the big grant-awarding foundations and most NGOs. But the subject is often lost amid a skein of confused and contradictory intentions: if sub-Saharan Africa's age pyramid is characterized by a 'youth bulge', what is the point of the innumerable 'youth-targeting projects'? Some 600 million Africans – half of the continent's population – do not constitute a 'target' so much as a chasm, and a bottomless one at that.

Recently, however, several books have opened up new ground on the subject. In France, as early as 2010, Jean-Michel Severino and Olivier Ray published *Le Temps de l'Afrique* (which appeared in English in 2011 as *Africa's Moment*). Their approach overall is optimistic, predicated on the hope that Africa will benefit from a 'demographic dividend' when its abundant youth population enters the workforce. In 2015, the French researcher Serge Michaïlof, a former senior advisor at the World Bank, wrote *Africanistan*, a book that is openly sceptical that a large number of African youth will find remunerative work, fearing instead that 'Africa's crisis will end up on our doorsteps' – a rough translation of the book's subtitle.[16] In the United States, Marc Sommer's *The Outcast Majority: War, Development, and Youth in Africa*, also published in 2015, amplified his expertise on African youth drawn from decades of fieldwork. Finally, Moussa Mara, Mali's prime minister from 2014 to 2015, and the youngest person in his country to hold that office, placed the demographic challenge squarely at the heart of his 2016 book *Jeunesse africaine, le grand défi à relever*. Broaching a subject that is normally taboo, Mara came out in favour of birth control, noting that with a growth rate of 3 per cent, the Malian economy must expand at a rate of 7 per cent annually over the next eighteen years if per capita GNP is going to double. And even if it does, Mali, whose per capita GNP in 2015 was 675 US dollars, will take more than a century to reach the *current* per capita GNP of France, now around 44,000 US dollars.

If the phrase 'African youth' is now almost a pleonasm, then human geography is of paramount importance for understanding contemporary Africa. Persistent poverty, political and economic struggles, armed conflicts, the rise of religious extremism, educational and environmental challenges, the 'stress test' between generations, as well as – the main subject of this book – the migratory rush towards Europe: all these are inextricably linked to the matrix of Africa's exceptionally young population, especially that of sub-Saharan Africa – a fact made more striking in the context of a wider world that is greying by the year. With that in mind, this book invites you to revisit what should arguably be called 'the island continent of Peter Pan'.

But first, a word of warning. On a continent where civil registries are generally inaccurate, where even the best bureaucracy – in South Africa – only manages to record (assuming this is even true) eight births and deaths for every ten (Malan 2012: 128), a continent where the first reliable census data is only from the 1950s or later (in Chad, the first population count was conducted in 1993), to ground arguments on statistics looks like a fool's errand. To use a decimal point is proof of a researcher's naivety, if not incompetence. Ghana revised its GDP upwards by 63 per cent in 2010; Nigeria by 89 per cent in 2013; and Kenya by 25 per cent in 2014, a mere one-quarter increase. . . . In one stroke of a computer key, a country's entire economic statistics can vault skyward. By the same token, when the media report a figure for the number of displaced persons in Africa, it is as well to remember that these people were not counted when they were still living, unperturbed, at home (Allison 2014). And what about the reported number of casualties in African wars? Are they not haphazard, often simply wild, extrapolations? The World Bank's chief economist, Shanta Devarajan, has deplored the 'statistical tragedy of Africa'.[17]

Adducing a host of examples from across the continent, the economist Morten Jerven has written a book – *Poor Numbers: How We Are Misled by African Development Statistics and What to Do About It* (2013) – to lay bare the fragile foundations on which Africa's temples of statistics are built. Jerven's argument is compelling, and there is little to add to his findings, other than that the kingdom of false data is only one province in a vast empire of bad faith. It is already a nearly insurmountable challenge to figure out how many people live on what daily budget in Africa. In 2011, struggling to identify the continent's middle class, the African Development Bank came up with a definition that included anyone enjoying a disposable income of 2 to 20 dollars

a day – some 327 million Africans, or about a third of the population between Tangiers and Cape Town.[18] Such good news! Once
you know that two-thirds of those falling into this income bracket
earn between 2 and 5 dollars a day, and that nowhere else in the
world would so little purchasing power be considered an entry
ticket into a middle class worthy of the name, it's clear that 'statistics' rhymes with 'politics'.

All the numerical data in this book, and there are plenty, have
been researched with the utmost care . . . and scepticism. They
are designed to provide scale, orders of magnitude and points of
comparison, for certain general realities and persistent trends.
They are not intended to conjure mathematical precision or even
the illusion of exactitude – which, in contemporary Africa, is far
beyond anyone's reach.

1

The Law of Large Numbers

Africa's demography shifted profoundly between the two world wars. For one thing, the continent had finally surmounted the 'microbial shock' that was an attendant circumstance of its colonization towards the end of the nineteenth century – more on this in a moment. For another, Africa's principal colonial powers, Great Britain and France, rushed to endow their overseas possessions with the infrastructure and public health services they had previously deemed unnecessary. Britain adopted the Colonial Development and Welfare Act in 1940, while France created its Fonds d'investissement pour le développement économique et social (FIDES) six years later. Although the concept of 'development' is widely viewed as a by-product of the Cold War – more realistically, it was a sort of 'geopolitical rent' paid to friendly regimes in the Third World – it actually has an older, colonial heritage. The American historian Frederick Cooper, who first wrote about this interwar shift and coined the expression 'developmental colonialism', argues that the turn taken in the 1930s aimed not only to increase exploitation, but to reframe Europe's 'civilizing mission' (Cooper 2002). The dominion over populations presented as being 'different', if not 'inferior', was now justified by the stated purpose of leading them out of under-development. The colonial powers were becoming defensive. In tilting their objective towards the well-being of their 'subjects', they were trying to re-legitimize their overseas presence. But this project had an unintended consequence: the newfound emphasis on development and public health would prompt the greatest demographic boom in human history.[1]

In the 1930s, Africa's population began its rapid rise. Clearly, there is a 'before' and an 'after' to that historical landmark. Before, as far back in history as we can reach, the continent's population growth had been barely measurable, if not stagnant, heavily impacted by two demographic catastrophes: the slave trades and the epidemiological impact of the 'colonial encounter'. After, Africa's population experienced the most astounding growth ever known – if current trends continue, it will have increased by a factor of 17 between 1930 and 2050. By comparison, the equivalent multiplier for the United Kingdom, whose population was about 45 million in 1930 and will be an estimated 77 million in 2050, is a mere 1.7, or ten times less. If the United Kingdom's population followed the African curve, the UK would have a population of some 725 million people by 2050, roughly half that of China today.

Before its demographic surge, the population of sub-Saharan Africa had grown by only 20 per cent between 1500 and 1900, from around 80 million to some 95 million inhabitants; during that same period the population of Europe, like that of China, had quintupled. Why this disparity? Sub-Saharan Africa's low population density, rudimentary agricultural practices, tropical diseases, lack of hygiene, high infant and maternal mortality were all contributing factors. But only one explanation cuts across the *longue durée* pattern of demographic languor in a continent with such a diversity of ecosystems and political structures as Africa: the slave trades.

The deportation of some 28 million enslaved Africans between the seventh and nineteenth centuries – more than a millennium – amounts to a demographic trauma for Africa south of the Sahara. Men, and to a lesser extent women and children, were dragged from their homes and communities along four distinct trafficking routes: inside sub-Saharan Africa, mostly as a result of local warfare; across the Sahara to North Africa and the Mediterranean; across the Indian Ocean as part of the so-called 'Arab' slave trade; and finally, across the Atlantic as part of the triangular trading system. In the latter case, ships sailed from Europe for Africa with fabrics, metals, pearls, guns and ammunition. These goods were traded for slaves, who were then transported to America – the second leg of the triangle, known as the 'Middle Passage'. In the New World, the human cargo was replaced by commodities from the region, above all sugar, which was then brought back and sold on the Old Continent, completing the triangle. Though the transatlantic trade had the shortest duration of all the slave trading schemes, lasting roughly from 1500 to about 1850, it was also the most intense, especially between 1650 and 1850. It was also the best organized and the best documented. It is estimated that about 12 million Africans were taken to the New World, most notably to the British and French West Indies (45 per cent), Brazil (30 per cent) and the Spanish-speaking Americas (10 per cent). The territory that is now the continental United States received fewer than 5 per cent of those sold into slavery (Knight 1996: 817). The main slave trading nations were Portugal and Great Britain, which respectively deported 4 and 3 million Africans from their continent. The long-term death rate during the Middle Passage was around 10 per cent, while the trek across the Sahara and towards the Mediterranean was the deadliest, costing the lives of one-fifth of those in captivity.

The mortality of the triangular slave trade has been calculated based on a comparison of the embarkation and disembarkation registries of some 3,000 transatlantic voyages. Taken together, there is documentation preserved for some 25,000 additional voyages, themselves a fraction of an unknown total number. So far, disembarkation records have been found for around 10,000 Middle Passage journeys, while there are only embarkation records for some additional 8,000 trips. Because sub-Saharan population estimates during the slave trade era are themselves extrapolations into the past – 'retropolations', so to speak – of censuses from the 1950s (the first with any reliability), it is easy to see how precarious any of these trafficking figures really are. Still, they are far more trustworthy than anything we can say about the impact of the 'microbial shock' that hit the continent in the late nineteenth century.

Beginning in 1492, the introduction of European pathogens into the Americas caused a demographic collapse so profound that an estimated nine-tenths of Amerindians perished in the next 100 years. To make up for the loss of the indigenous labour force and maintain the profitability of their plantations, particularly sugar cane, the Portuguese, soon followed by other European powers, turned to Africa for slaves. Africans were slightly less vulnerable to smallpox, influenza, measles or typhus epidemics, in part because they had built up some immunity since Europeans began to arrive on Africa's West Coast in the fifteenth century (after the introduction of the caravel, a smaller, more agile ship that was able to sail against the prevailing trade winds). Yet the vast majority of Africans, especially in the interior, were utterly unprepared for the microbial and viral shock of the 'colonial encounter' in the second half of the nineteenth century. The geographer Sylvie Brunel believes that European colonization resulted in the deaths of 'one quarter of the population of central Africa in the nineteenth century from disease, massacres and forced displacement, which stripped many Africans of their natural protection against malaria' (2014: loc. 1236).[2] The historian Catherine Coquery-Vidrovitch estimates that by 1921, French Equatorial Africa (AEF) – the federation of French colonies in central Africa – had lost one-third of its population (1985: 46–64). Adam Hochschild, the author of *King Leopold's Ghost*, holds that half the population, not just in the former Belgian Congo, but across all of equatorial Africa, succumbed to widespread epidemics (1998: 273, 328–9). However, it is impossible to reach any verifiable conclusions. Whatever the extent of the human destruction, the data are simply not that reliable or detailed. It is generally believed that half of all Central Africans and a third of all West Africans perished between 1880 and 1930, a demographic catastrophe comparable to the bubonic plague in Europe: in the fourteenth century, the 'Black Death' killed between 30 and 50 per cent of Europe's population.

Africa: The World's Youth

After a millennium of demographic stagnation, Africa was faced with two cataclysms – the slave trades and colonization – all of this before the continent began its stupendous growth spurt starting in the 1930s. By then, some 150 million people lived in Africa, constituting about 13 per cent of the world's population. In 1650, prior to the decimations of the slave trades and the microbial shock, some 100 million people lived on the continent, or about one person out of every five worldwide. Between those two periods, and especially after 1750 when Europe entered its industrial revolution, the world population began to increase more and more rapidly.[3] Eighty-five per cent of the world's population growth has occurred since 1800 – a mere 0.02 per cent of the time humans have walked the earth – and it was not until 1800 that the world's population even reached 1 billion. It then took a mere 130 years to reach 2 billion; and a further thirty years, until 1960, to add another billion. From that 3 billion mark in 1960, the world's population more than doubled in fifty years, reaching 7 billion inhabitants by 2010. By 2024, another billion people will have been added.

Despite this prodigious rise, global population decline is already underway. The world reached the zenith of its fertility at the end of the 1960s, having experienced the strongest surge in absolute numbers while that generation came of age in the 1980s.

Every year, during the 1980s, 85 million newborns were added to the world's population; within a dozen years another billion people had joined the planet. Since then, not only are the world's most developed countries – with Japan in the lead – ageing rapidly, but Latin America and a large part of Asia are 'greying' in tandem. The pill and other modern contraceptives have accelerated this trend. In some cases, they have even contributed, along with other factors, to a drop in population growth below the statistical replacement rate of 2.1 children per woman of childbearing age. Several developed countries – not only Japan but also Germany, Greece, Italy and Spain – have entered the historically uncharted territory of negative population growth in the absence of natural disasters or pandemics. They are now experiencing a demographic 'paradox of plenty': in the midst of material abundance, their inhabitants show a dwindling desire for children.

Conspicuously absent from the media-driven population debate, but perhaps even more important than the reproductive revolution, are the constant gains in longevity achieved since the beginning of the twentieth century. In 1900, life expectancy in both Europe and North America was forty-seven years; by 1950 it had leapt to seventy years. Today, that seventy is the worldwide average, and life in retirement – the 'third age', after youth and adulthood – is seen as a time of vitality and opportunity.

On a generally 'greying' planet, Africa is becoming the exception to the demographic rule. Its sub-Saharan share of global population is the most 'youthful' part of the world and the only region where the population will continue to increase between 2.5 and 3 per cent from now until 2050, a pace even more rapid than when the world was at the apex of its population growth. Sub-Saharan Africa's growth jump from 150 million in 1930 to 300 million in 1960 – when the UN proclaimed a 'Year of Africa' as seventeen colonies south of the Sahara became independent – was followed by further growth: the population had doubled again by the time the Cold War ended in 1989. In 2010 it reached 1 billion. By 2050, Africa's population is expected to reach 2.5 billion.

By then, it will be roughly a quarter of the world's population of 10 billion. By 2100, that proportion will have doubled once again, and Africans will represent some 40 per cent of the world's anticipated population of 11 billion. Even more significantly, about 60 per cent of all people under the age of fifteen will live south of the Sahara: a solid majority of the world's youth will be African.

The price of what is available in abundance depreciates, while scarcity increases value. That rule applies today for young people in a world predominantly populated by older adults, as it applied yesterday in Africa, a historically underpopulated continent of 30 million square kilometres, more than three times the size of Europe from Vladivostok to Gibraltar. In 1650, Africa's population density averaged 3.3 inhabitants per square kilometre compared with forty-five per square kilometre today, and twice as many in 2050 if current trends prevail. Until the dawn of the twentieth century, the continent's population was its most precious public good, while land was so abundant that it scarcely counted as a factor of production in comparison to human capital. As a result, 'wealth-in-people' hoarded by lineage-bonded societies – which claim descent from a common ancestor – was the driving force of African history. With this in mind, the African participation in the slave trades could be seen as the functional equivalent of 'scorched earth' policies in Europe where, by contrast, the ownership of land – land tenure – has long been the motor of history. In Africa, as we have seen, this *longue durée* pattern came to an end in the 1930s due to a demographic reversal of fortunes. Cynically speaking, the value of human life has declined in inverse proportion to the continent's unprecedented population growth (even though the population density of Africa is still low compared with other parts of the world[4]). Conversely, African land is more and more coveted.

Even with the benefit of hindsight, the effects of Africa's demographic surge are often hidden in plain sight. This makes the perspicacity of a former British Governor of Nigeria – who *predicted* the consequences of exponential population growth and translated them into policy recommendations – all the more remarkable. In 1955, in a missive sent to London on the subject of universal primary education – the flagship programme that the metropolis wanted to put into place to help counteract the swelling pro-independence tide – he pointed out that the rapid population growth underway was going to make it too costly for the British government to finance free education for everyone. Bucking the strategy of 'holding on' to the colonies, the Governor recommended instead speeding up the date of Nigeria's independence. 'Inevitably, people will be disappointed', he argued, 'and it's better they be disappointed by the failure of their own leaders than by our actions' (quoted in Cooper 2002: 76).

A good half century later, the realpolitik inherent in this observation is rarely matched. Indeed, we spend our time evaluating and re-evaluating the legacy of African independence, focusing on the 'corruption' and 'mismanagement' of various governments, without adding that satisfying the need for public goods and infrastructure of an exponentially growing population wasn't a viable proposition in the first place. Unlike the British Governor, we prefer moral lessons to insights. In a society where each new generation is more populous than the last, efforts to build enough housing, roads, schools and hospitals are bound to fail. What the French economist Alfred Sauvy called 'demographic investments' will inevitably fall short because, no matter how hard one tries, there will never be enough for everyone. In this context, to secure something for oneself, one's kin or ethnic group – whether a minister seeking a kickback from a foreign investor or a policeman extorting a petty bribe at a roadblock – is merely a rational choice. In fact, it is the same rational choice that the entire population is making by grudgingly accepting this informal taxation as the price to pay for allowing a few exceptions to the country's general penury. Of course, this is not an example of moral or ethical conduct, any more than the former British Governor's analysis was directed at improving the future of Africa at the expense of Her Majesty's government. But, instead of insisting on the moral depravity of corruption, we would gain from understanding how corruption becomes the currency – the coin of the realm – in a market where there is an abysmal mismatch between supply and demand, and no coercive regulatory force to prevent bending the rules. Because, by recommending our own 'virtuousness' to people living in circumstances that we do not know, we risk being perceived like the archetypal Dickensian hypocrite, Seth Pecksniff – 'a direction-post, which is always telling the way to a place, and never goes there'.

Nigeria: Take It or Leave It

In the mid-1980s, I was given the opportunity to make some extra money in Lagos, which was then the capital of the Federal Republic of Nigeria (Abuja, built from scratch in the centre of the country, became the official capital only in 1991). I had already been visiting Lagos regularly from my base in neighbouring Benin, although I never had the means to stay there as long as I would have wanted. The *per diem* from Radio France International (RFI), where I worked as a freelancer covering West Africa, was just enough to pay for my transport costs and rent a 'guest room' on the premises of a French construction company – a bare-bones lodging consisting of four cinderblock walls. The white, industrial bread that I ate – a bit like sweetened foam rubber cut into small oblong blocks that sat beneath a sheet of plastic and was constantly wet from condensation in the intense humidity – had become my staple diet. I wanted to be permanently based in Lagos, but this dream was not within my reach. Just the cost of a secure office, even one that doubled as my home, a diesel generator and an international telephone line safe from regular switch-offs and ransom attempts, far exceeded the monetary value of my journalistic work. All this is to say that I was delighted when the Lagos bureau chief of Reuters News Agency asked me to help them out.

At the time, Lagos was a city of about 5 million people. I had fallen for this singular urban space, built along the Atlantic Ocean and around a string of interconnected lagoons. Numerous bridges linked the islands to the mainland. There were slums beneath the bridges, and a row of skyscrapers stood out like a cordillera along the marina – a sight then still rare in sub-Saharan Africa. I loved how nightfall would come, like a velvet curtain falling; when the city lights began to glisten on the water, young women hastily unpacked their high heels from plastic bags, put them on straining for balance and laughing out loud, eager to join the dance floor. I loved listening to the Afro-Beat of Fela Anikulapo Kuti in The Shrine, his nightspot and the heart of popular resistance to the country's military dictatorship headed by General Muhammadu Buhari (now a 'convert' to democracy, who was elected president again in 2015). Looking back, I think I also, and perhaps especially, loved Lagos because so many expatriates abhorred it: 'a cesspool of violence and corruption', 'pandemonium!' I believed myself exceptional because I was exceptionally at ease in an Africa where my days disappeared into the giant traffic jams known as 'go-slows', and I sat in the back of a dilapidated taxi in the fetid heat in high spirits. At night, I took pride when the flashlights at the checkpoints ceased to blind me and, out of the dark, obscure silhouettes muttering under their breath with dissatisfaction, and sometimes insults, gradually emerged. The pungent scent of fermented palm wine, the official aroma of the police and soldiers armed with assault rifles, wafted through the lowered windows. I held my ground, I gave up nothing. Calm returned until the next checkpoint, never far away. It was a game, a rite of passage: run the gauntlet without getting hit.

Reuters hired me to help them compile their annual report on Nigeria, a statistical directory prefaced by an overview of larger trends in the local economy. The Reuters bureau chief, Nick Kotch, took care of that section and did so with style; I was tasked with the drudgery of unearthing run-of-the-mill stats, and the harder job of trying to corroborate them. Yet any statistic would almost always be predicated on the population figures in Africa's most populous country. That wouldn't have been a problem if the military regimes had not suppressed the census data they knew was a source of national discord. The last population count dated from 1973 and had been rejected by the country's political leaders. Both the north and the south, rivals for the control of the federal government, the country's one-stop shopping centre for power and money, challenged the 1973 figures as they had challenged the census of 1962, the first after Nigeria's independence. Great Britain had been conducting population counts since 1866, initially in its small 'colony of Lagos', then in all of Nigeria after the 'amalgamation' of the northern and southern regions in 1914, when the country's modern-day boundaries were established. Census takers had to contend with everything from locust invasions to riots against a head tax, which Nigerians resisted with the same intensity as grasshopper swarms. During the 1952 census, under colonial rule, Nigerians were intent on keeping the total population count as low as possible to minimize taxation; once they had become citizens of their own country, however, they adapted the opposite strategy, each region trying to magnify its numbers during the 1962 count to gain more traction at the federal level – there were legislative seats assigned on the basis of population, as well as investments and subsidies. It was rumoured that the north had been counting its goats and sheep as citizens. Finally, in 1976, the government 'adjusted' its demographic growth rate. With the stroke of a pen, a population that had been growing at a 2.5 per cent clip was now growing at 3.2 per cent.

As it happened, the calculations were constantly being refigured from a new and arbitrary base, each successive manoeuvre compounding the initial errors. Despite our best efforts, our report on Nigeria was a distortion of the real picture. From GDP per capita through the poverty index to food self-sufficiency, every figure had to be viewed with the utmost circumspection. And not much has changed since then. In 1991, amid the excitement of a return to democracy, a 'transparent' census was held which pegged the country's population at 88 million inhabitants

– a blatant underestimation in the eyes of the World Bank, which rejected the count and came up with its own figure of 99.9 million (an attempt at precision which struck me as absurd). Then, after the 2006 census, the last to date, another General and ex-putschist, Olusegun Obasanjo, came to power by the ballot box. His advice in colloquial Nigerian to anyone contesting the census results: 'If you like, use am, if you no like, leave am.'

This 'take it or leave it' attitude challenges all the statistical directories and, lately, entire databanks devoted to Nigeria. But agnosticism is unaffordable in a country that is the demographic laboratory of sub-Saharan Africa. Its population, supposedly around 40 million people in 1960, had tripled by the year 2000. Its roughly 150 million inhabitants in 2010 equalled the population of the whole of sub-Saharan Africa in 1930. Today, according to the CIA's *World Factbook*, Nigeria has around 190 million inhabitants. As for its anticipated population in 2050, the figures have varied widely but have been invariably underestimated over the course of the last decade. For instance, in 2008 the US Population Reference Bureau put them at 282 million, two years later at 326 million, and in 2015 at 397 million. In the absence of reliable benchmarks, the findings gleaned from a number of in-depth studies must also be taken lightly: based on the best available data, the country's fertility rate has dropped from 6.8 children in 1975 to 5.5 children for each woman of child-bearing age. Yet this slow decline masks important regional differences. The birth rate in the south has fallen sharply, while in the predominantly Muslim north, the fertility rate has increased, reaching 7.3 children for each woman of reproductive age. In some northern states, the percentage of women who use modern contraceptives is closer to 5 per cent than 10, and women can only visit family planning clinics accompanied by a man – their husband, father, an uncle or a brother. In 2012, across the entire country, life expectancy stood at fifty-two years, two-thirds of the life expectancy in the UK, where it was eighty-one. The maternal death rate during childbirth has barely shifted since 1975; infant mortality has fallen, although at seventy-eight deaths per 1,000 live births, it still languishes at a level which the world's most industrialized countries reached a century ago.

Almost all of sub-Saharan Africa, with the notable exception of South Africa, bears a striking resemblance to Nigeria. Despite some variation throughout the region and, in some cases, inside a single country, exponential population growth has continued unabated south of the Sahara since the first half of the twentieth century. Due to this fact, even a drop in infant mortality by 50 per cent since 1990 looks like a deterioration: prior to 1990, a third of all infants worldwide who died before the age of one were born in Africa; today, it is half of them. The decline in infant mortality south of the Sahara has not yet been accompanied by a corresponding drop in the fertility rate. Meanwhile, maternal mortality also remains very high: 546 mothers die for every 100,000 live births, according to UNICEF, compared with eight per 100,000 in the United Kingdom and sixteen in the United States. Nonetheless, between now and 2050, twenty-eight sub-Saharan countries will see their populations double, while nine others – Angola, Burundi, Malawi, Mali, Niger, Somalia, Uganda, Tanzania and Zambia – will see their populations quintuple. As a result, between now and 2100, three out of every four newborns in the world will be born in sub-Saharan Africa (Null 2011).[5]

Lagos: Half Paradise, Half Slum

In his 2004 novel, *GraceLand*, the Nigerian writer Chris Abani tells the story of a young man, Elvis Oke, who lives in the city's largest slum area, built on stilts in the lagoon under West Africa's most travelled bridge. In the Nigerian megacity, nothing is purely local, nothing is purely foreign. Everything is 'remotely global' (Piot 1999). The title of the novel and the name of the protagonist refer to Elvis Presley and his residence in Memphis, Tennessee, transformed since 1982 into a museum for the American rock 'n' roll idol. The Nigerian Elvis tries to earn a living by impersonating his celebrity namesake, whose existence he discovered on a postcard. He has read, though it's not clear how, Rainer Maria Rilke's *Letters to a Young Poet*, and reckons that Dickens' *A Tale of Two Cities* is a 'perfect description of life in Lagos'.

Elvis Oke comes from a village in the southeast of Nigeria, in Igboland. He was raised by his grandmother after his mother died of cancer when he was eight years old. Only his grandmother expresses the belief, in local English, that 'children are never too young to hear tha truth'. To the other grown-ups, Elvis is just a kid who has nothing of interest to say to his elders, seniority – the privilege of age – being the operative, sacrosanct principle in the village. That is, until the day of Elvis's initiation, when a circle of kaolin is traced around his neck, the mark of the future head of the family, and he is urged to 'look death in the face'. For the girls, a circle is traced around the elbow, which they must henceforth bend willingly in hard work.

Elvis is little more than ten years old when he quits school to go and live with Sunday, his father, in Lagos. Is he escaping the countryside he knows all too well or is he attracted by the city's bright lights? The question doesn't come up as he delves into 'the whirl of urban life'. The village remains his permanent reference, though it only survives in half-extinguished memories. Lagos is for Elvis not a home but a hybrid, a living monster that is 'half slum, half paradise, hideous and violent, yet beautiful at the same time'. His alcoholic father, remarried and now responsible for three more children, is of little help. Sunday invested in modernity but has been poorly repaid. He financed the studies of his older brother who, having made his fortune, didn't honour his debt. This breach of two fundamental rules, one of birthright and the other of reciprocity, has ruined Sunday's existence.

Life in a Lagos slum is a *War of the Buttons*: in the 1912 novel by Louis Pergaud, which has been adapted for the cinema in both French and English productions, two groups of schoolboys from rival villages constantly face off against each other, with results ranging from a good fist fight to a nasty murder. But in the fictional account, it is enough for Tigibus – *petit Gibus* – to utter 'Okay, my man, if I had known, I wouldn't have come' to call it quits. Elvis, by contrast, is set on a path that ultimately destroys him. Imitating his American idol doesn't teach him how to survive. Instead, he is lured by his buddy and mentor, Redemption, into a game of criminal one-upmanship, starting with simple theft and moving on to human trafficking, child prostitution, torture and murder. The unsentimental education of Elvis – the Nigerian version of *Emile*, Jean-Jacques Rousseau's 1762 nature-of-man treatise – is a coming-of-age story in which parental authority, and, more generally, the influence of elders, no longer exist. For him and his companions in Lagos, the only guiding spirit in their unsettled life is a self-proclaimed 'King of Beggars'. But the wise old ruler, a rare celestial body in their dark firmament, is threatened with extinction in a galaxy of young people.

Lagos is the 'Big Bang' of African youth, its official birthplace. It was here that the British authorities defined a new age-grouping – between fourteen and eighteen years old. This administrative category represented a clear departure from the precolonial order, which recognized those who had undergone initiation and those who had not, with no intermediate category of 'adolescence'. In other words, one was either a child or an adult. In Europe, with a more complex division of labour wrought by the Industrial Revolution, an intermediate stage of life became necessary: between childhood and adulthood, a parenthesis was opened and filled with all manner of education, including long years of book learning, well beyond the mere imitative emulation of parents in the field or workshop that had been the norm in previous centuries. In Lagos, however, 'youth' came into being as a cohort that needed to be closely monitored by the police, a collection of youngsters hanging around in small groups in areas in town known as either 'bases' or 'junctions': in the bases they killed time; in the junctions they concocted schemes to make easy money (Ismail 2009). Political violence, outsourced to 'area boys' by Nigeria's ruling class, has always been part of their livelihood.

Lagos is an old city with a growing proportion of young people. In 1921, 62 per cent of its inhabitants were less than thirty years old; in 1972, that figure was 78 per cent. Today, in the shanty towns filled with the youngsters leaving the rural areas en masse – at a rate of some 600,000 a year – the proportion of under-thirties is nearly 95 per cent. As they get older, they either escape the slum, or die in it, or return to their villages as failures, fallen angels of a new and better world. As a result, in the blighted parts of Lagos where two-thirds of its inhabitants live, the age pyramid has been essentially flattened: young people live among young people, reinventing norms and customizing values to fit their situation. It is not necessarily the *Lord of the Flies* but it is hardly a rulebook for civic-mindedness. In any event, passing moral judgement is as difficult as drawing a straight line in a curved universe – and not only in Lagos. The famous 419 fraud letters – a scam known around the world and named for the section of the Nigerian penal code that punishes email fraud – emanate from urban slums such as the one Elvis lives in; yet this type of swindle, whose fulsome promises of a 'reward' strain credulity, only work because of the greed of foreign bank account holders who are ready to send large sums of money to any dubious address in expectation of a hefty return.

The rural exodus tells only half of the story. 'Urban magnetism' is just as powerful a force. Together they explain why sub-Saharan African cities are growing even more rapidly than their respective countries' populations as a whole. At independence in 1960, Lagos had some 350,000 inhabitants; in the mid-1980s, when I first ventured into the tangle of African statistics, the city had a population of some 5 million. In 2012 Lagos overtook Cairo as Africa's most populous city, with 21 million people, a number expected to double by 2050. It bears reiterating that this once mid-size town ballooning into a megacity continues to grow younger. The percentage of inhabitants less than fifteen years old surpassed 25 per cent in 1930, rose to near 40 per cent at independence, and today oscillates around 60 per cent, a figure that makes Lagos the unquestioned world citadel of youth. A comparison with Inner London or downtown Paris puts its youthfulness into perspective, just as it throws the ageing – even the mummification – of European capitals into stark relief: in London and Paris, the proportion of inhabitants who are under fifteen is, respectively, 18 and 14 per cent.

But it is not only the age difference that creates this yawning chasm. If one were to count only the people with access to European-style infrastructure, Nigeria's megacity would have the population of a ghost town. To take just one example, in 2006, Lagos had some 15 million inhabitants, but just 0.4 per cent of the city's toilets were connected to a central sewage system (Packer 2006). And despite some progress, the Lagos lagoon remains a cloaca – flushed only by tides and rainfall – where most residents wash and get their drinking and cooking water. Little wonder, then, that the local welcome – *This is Lagos!* – sounds like a warning. Affluent Lagosians are seeking to live in the futuristic offshore city Eko Atlantic, 10 square kilometres of land that have been reclaimed from the Atlantic thanks to millions of cubic metres of rock dumped into the sea since 2012.[6] Some 250,000 people are expected to one day live here, reliably connected to the internet via a transatlantic fibre-optic cable and to the outside world thanks to helicopter drop-offs at Murtala Muhammed International Airport.

Since independence in 1960, Nigeria's population has increased more than fourfold, but the number of Lagosians has jumped by a factor of . . . 60! The demographic growth rate of Africa's most populous nation corresponds more or less to the average rate of growth of all countries south of the Sahara. However, the expansion of Lagos, due also to vigorous migration into the city from neighbouring countries, is exceptional, between two and four times the urban growth rate of 'ordinary' sub-Saharan cities. Still, Abidjan, the other West African city attracting a large number of regional migrants, has also increased its population fortyfold since 1960; and N'Djamena, with only 23,000 inhabitants in 1960, compared with 1.3 million today, is just behind Lagos, with a growth factor of 55 due exclusively to a massive rural exodus. The populations of Dakar, Freetown, Nairobi and Harare have increased by factors of ten to fifteen over the same period. Bamako, Khartoum and Mogadishu have expanded around twenty times, while Conakry, Kampala, Kinshasa and Ouagadougou have grown by a factor of 30.

Urbanization south of the Sahara has been so extraordinary – historically unmatched both in scope and pace – partly because it started at such a low level. Of course, there have always been cities in sub-Saharan Africa. But in 1920, the rate of urbanization was 2.5 per cent and 40 per cent of the continent's city dwellers lived in the Yoruba region in southwest Nigeria alone. In 1940, there were only six cities south of the Sahara with more than 100,000 inhabitants: Ibadan, Addis Ababa, Kano, Lagos, Accra and Dakar. They contained, all together, about 1 million people. Today, there are forty sub-Saharan cities with at least a million people. In 2008, while the number of urban dwellers worldwide for the first time surpassed those living in rural areas, about 35 per cent of Africans lived in cities, according to the African Development Bank. By 2030, city dwellers will be the majority in Africa as well. And in 2050, around 60 per cent of Africa's population – some 1.25 billion people – will live in cities like Lagos. Put differently: between 1960 and 2000, Africa's urban population surged by 8.7 times; by 2050 it will have quadrupled again.

The Chinese Model

Runaway population growth, increasing youthfulness and landslide urbanization – all three in proportions unprecedented in human history – have been the demographic features of Africa for almost a century. Faced with these realities and their many challenges, three attitudes have prevailed: a lack of attention to the issue, blank denial or a ham-fisted approach. Inattention has stifled curiosity and resulted in ignorance. Between 1970 and 2000, of thirty-nine major studies worldwide focusing on the link between demographics and poverty, only six were conducted in countries south of the Sahara (Tabutin 2007: 261). Denial has expressed itself in remarks like those made in a 2015 BBC interview with Swedish Professor Hans Rosling, perhaps the world's best-known statistician. According to Rosling, 'if you continue to have extreme poverty areas where women give birth to six children and the population doubles in one generation, then you will have problems. But it's not the population growth that is the problem – it's the extreme poverty that is the underlying reason.'[7] Finally, a maladroit approach has consisted in dismissing what, historically, has constituted Africa's most valued asset: 'wealth-in-people', the term coined by anthropologists to emphasize the importance of kinship ties and social affiliations in achieving status, power and influence. So, stoking neo-Malthusian fears because of 'too many Africans', or warning that a 'demographic bomb' has been detonated on their continent, or fulminating against a 'glut' of young sub-Saharans who are likely to 'invade' Europe, can hardly resonate positively with Africans. Besides, it is a misrepresentation of Africa's demographic challenge. The number of Africans, and the population age structure on their continent, are not per se problematic. They only become a problem when the social organization and its corollary, productivity, do not allow for a basic quality of life, of housing, of education and of care-giving to those in need; when the sheer number of people makes the well-being of each one impossible given the available resources. In the words of the American Constitution: most African countries are set up for failure in their 'pursuit of happiness'.

In 1958, a demographer named Ansley Coale and an economist named Edgar Hoover put forth a hypothesis on the link between population and prosperity. Unlike much of what had been written before or since, they did not focus on the size of a population or its growth rate. What interested them was not the height or the width of the age pyramid, but its proportion. In their eyes, the proportion was 'good' when it created the optimum amount of wealth to share, which meant that the ratio between working-age adults and dependants – the retired elderly as well as the under-age young – favoured those in the workforce. Viewed from this perspective, a lowering of the fertility rate in Africa would change the situation for the better in four ways. First, there would be an increase in the amount of wealth to share among all members of society if the working-age population no longer had to support, in addition to itself and elderly relatives, an ever greater number of minors. Second, there would be an increase in the savings rate in both the private and public sector, since per capita spending would decline in both areas. This would permit, thirdly, an increase in investments in human capital, again as much at home as in the public domain, thanks to more money available to spend on education. Finally, wages and salaries would rise in tandem with fewer and fewer young people entering the labour market.

It is worth noting that the 'demographic bonus' or 'demographic dividend' that is accrued with a bulge in the working-age population is not counted among the specific advantages enumerated by Coale and Hoover. In fact, the integration into the workforce of greater numbers of young people is never a given ahead of time because job creation is not a simple act of volition by employers or governments. Even in the case of full employment, the increased wealth is only a temporary windfall since this larger cohort of employees will one day leave their jobs and retire. In the absence of an equal number of young successors, their retirement will create an unfavourable ratio of working adults to dependants – a 'demographic malus' that offsets the ephemeral bonus.

This is one of the reasons, though it is rarely discussed, why China's one-child policy, which was officially rescinded on 1 January 2016, does not provide a model for Africa. Initially, it was a success: between 1965 and 2015 the ratio between dependants

– those less than fifteen or more than sixty-five years old – and working adults went from 81 per cent to 37 per cent. In other words, in 2015, a hundred working-age adults were supporting just thirty-seven minors and retirees. That, along with many other factors, especially political, allowed hundreds of millions of Chinese to escape the so-called low-income, high-fertility trap. But despite appreciable gain for several generations, the one-child policy is ultimately a zero-sum game. The 'demographic bonus' that was the result of its inception in 1979 has already started to turn on itself with a vengeance. Since 2014, the ratio between working-age adults and their dependants has been deteriorating once again, since there are not enough young people to replace the vast numbers of the working population who have since moved into retirement. In 2060, it will be as unfavourable as it was in 1965, when every 100 working-age people had to support, in addition to themselves, eighty-one minors and retirees. The median age in China will climb to fifty years, in line with Germany, Spain and Japan (the median age in the United Kingdom and the US will be, respectively, a mere forty-four and forty-two years). And unlike the 'older' industrialized countries, China has not had time to build a collective retirement system. In addition, its traditional social network, known as *guanxi*, which relies on the solidarity of the extended family, has been unravelling for forty years. How to escape this new demographic trap, then, seems all the more complex. Though there are no longer state-level constraints on child-bearing, China's only children – nicknamed 'little Emperors' and, if they return to their parents' home, 'boomerang kids' – tend to only have one child themselves.[8] This reinforces the burdensome '4–2–1 syndrome', the responsibility that a single child carries in supporting two parents and four grandparents.

Of course, leaving aside these long-term trends, the overriding reason that disqualifies the Chinese model is its intrinsically coercive nature. Beijing imposed on Chinese parents what is elsewhere an intensely personal choice, terminating 336 million pregnancies

– roughly the current population of the United States. This policy will have a long-lasting impact on the demographic equilibrium between the sexes. Although in 1994 the government banned the use of sonography to determine the sex of a foetus and prevent the abortion of baby girls, today there are 35 million more boys than girls in China among those less than twenty years old.

Demographic Governance

Beginning in 1967, Kenya, and then Ghana three years later, were the first sub-Saharan African countries to adopt family planning policies. But the measures taken were far too timid to make much difference: since then Ghana's population has increased 3.5 times while Kenya's has quintupled. Moreover, the two countries remained an isolated vanguard for twenty years. It was only in 1988 that Nigeria, Senegal and Liberia followed suit. Over the next decade, thirty other countries joined them, not always out of genuine conviction, however, but rather because they wanted, or needed, to keep their external aid lenders satisfied.[9] Europe, the continent of Africa's former colonizers and its main purveyor of aid, has been mostly silent on issues concerning birth control in Africa. Indeed, a reluctance to deal frankly with this subject persists. At the press conference ending the G20 meeting in Hamburg on 8 July 2017, French president Emmanuel Macron stated the obvious: 'As long as women in some countries bear seven or eight children, you can decide to spend billions of euros there, but you're not going to stabilize anything.' Yet his statement unleashed a storm of indignation on social media and ignited a debate – not about the nexus between poverty and demography but about Macron's 'racism'. His candour was unusual. More typical are the comments of Serge Michaïlof, a research associate at IRIS, the leading French think tank on foreign policy, and the former executive director of the French development agency (AFD). He reproaches African governments for their lack of purpose in formulating public policies to curb population growth, then adds that there needs to be a 'total reworking of the language, the messaging, the projects themselves, of course done with great care and respecting each country's cultural heritage, without head-on confrontation, but resolutely' (Michaïlof 2015: 57). Yet, how do you square a total reset of family planning in Africa with full respect for the continental cultures? It is a contradiction in terms.

'For a long time, sub-Saharan Africa has shown a laissez-faire attitude, a disinterest, regarding demographic questions', observed John May, then the World Bank's Africa demographer, in 2007.[10] In the 1950s and 1960s, at a time when Africa needed to deal with this challenge in a decisive manner, Tunisian president Habib Bourguiba was the only leader to promote the transition to another family model against the headwinds of his times: his family code replaced repudiation with divorce, prohibited polygamy, required the bride's consent to her marriage, removed the obstacle of paternal consent and instituted equality not only between fathers and mothers but between their male and female children. However, such leadership was exceptional. Tanzania's president Julius Nyerere spoke for most of his fellow 'fathers of independence' when he said that, had he not taken his people where they wanted to go, his head would have rolled 'just as surely as the tickbird follows the rhino'.[11] In the general euphoria that accompanied Africa's accession to sovereignty, the new leaders found it politically difficult, if not suicidal, to challenge something as fundamental as reproductive habits; at a moment when everything seemed possible, discouraging procreation would have looked like spoiling the party. Besides, these new African states, even younger than their citizens, might have lacked the institutional capacity to enact such 'biopolitics', to use Michel Foucault's term. To this day, there remains an ad hoc quality to family planning south of the Sahara, where the use of modern methods of birth control – always less than 15 per cent among women of child-bearing age – has grown only slowly, year after year, in stark contrast to Asia, where the figure is more than 60 per cent.

If the former British Governor of Nigeria were given a second life to spend somewhere in Africa between the Tropics of Cancer and Capricorn, he would most certainly sound a warning about the next landslide in the region's human geography – the over-abundance of elderly people with no pension or social security, and no recourse to 'African solidarity', which will have run its course. But who cares about drought in the middle of a driv-ing rain? Old age in Africa seems to be nothing to worry about today, tomorrow, or even the day after. For now, as for nearly a century, the same mindset prevails. The colonial authorities, and then independent African governments themselves, have not engaged in demographic governance, at least not governance with any kind of foresight. Africa's population has increased at a rate never before seen in human history, *and* without a 'Green Revolution' to accompany it and offer a measure of food security. Hundreds of millions of people have left their villages; although they are themselves industrious, they have moved into cities with no industry, where they manage their lives, such as they are, on a day-to-day basis.

In contemporary Africa, in particular south of the Sahara, world records of youthfulness have been broken. In the next chapter, we will explore more closely this island-continent of Peter Pan. So many young people could hold out the promise of a bright future – provided a large percentage of them don't die in infancy, or from easily curable diseases, or in massacres or wars; provided, too, that vast numbers of them are not unemployed and unable to mature and fulfil their own personal potential. Africans have moved at a heroic rate to master the forms and institutions of modernity that once oppressed them, as we shall see in more detail shortly. But that progress has been set back, again and again, by the sheer weight of the continent's population. Such is the law of large numbers.

2

The Island-Continent of Peter Pan

In February 1994, an alarmist, dangerously catch-all and pro-
phetically headlined article appeared in *The Atlantic*, an American
monthly. Robert Kaplan's 'The Coming Anarchy: How scarcity,
crime, overpopulation, tribalism, and disease are rapidly destroying the social fabric of our planet' resonated with such force that
the US Department of State faxed it to every one of its embassies
in sub-Saharan Africa. Kaplan predicted a 'total crisis' in Africa
south of the Sahara, caused by violent crime, uncontrollable
epidemics and ecological disasters on the heels of Malthusian
population growth; its fallout would spell doomsday for the rest
of the world. The impact of Kaplan's reportage, which sparked
fierce controversy, was inseparable from the context in which it
was published. The world's hopes, raised by the end of the Cold
War, had been quickly dashed, and hard. After the fall of the
Berlin Wall in 1989, Francis Fukuyama had heralded 'the end
of history' as we knew it, a succession of power struggles and
grand strategies, and the advent of 'the last man', the prototypical
democrat flourishing in a liberal, market-driven economy. In this
optimistic scenario, Africa ceased to be a geopolitical backyard,

where the superpowers had averted a Third World War but at the cost of a series of wars in the Third World. Even in sub-Saharan Africa, life was no longer going to be Hobbesian, 'solitary, poor, nasty, brutish, and short'.

Very quickly, however, a cluster of new conflicts broke out, from Liberia to the Balkans by way of Sierra Leone and Somalia. They were waged against 'Otherness' and pitted so-called 'warlords' against each other in a scramble for loot, redefining 'civil' war as the massacre of civilians. These harsh realities gutted the hope for universal prosperity and perpetual peace that the end of the Cold War had promised. In 1993, Samuel Huntington explained these crises in terms of a 'clash of civilizations', in which cultural and religious identities would become the main source of post-Cold War confrontation. In April 1994, just two months after 'The Coming Anarchy' had appeared in print, Rwanda's 100-day genocide began. Exterminatory violence in Rwanda – *The Machete Season*[1] – exceeded even Kaplan's predictions.

A quarter-century later, the imminent apocalypse portrayed in Kaplan's article has lost much of its sombre potency. It is now clear that the author's 'fear of the dark' prevented him from realizing that the population increase in Africa – along with a massive rural exodus, hyper-rapid urbanization and the continent's accelerated insertion into the world economy – entailed not only grave risks but also previously unimagined opportunities. In retrospect, the blanket contempt with which Kaplan invalidated 'a lot of superficial Islam and superficial Christianity . . . undermined by animist beliefs not suitable to a moral society because they are based on irrational spirit power', while celebrating the Islam of North Africa or the Balkans as a 'social anchor', has become contemptible in its turn. Yet, in fairness, the academic discourse that posited 'Black Islam' as supposedly more tolerant than the volatile and often politically manipulated faith of the 'Arab street' has not stood the test of time either. Home-grown Islamist terrorist movements have sprung up across the entire Sahel region, from Mali through northern Nigeria to Somalia. And despite his sweeping generalizations, Kaplan deserves credit for having been among the first to draw attention to the importance of 'ordinary crime' in the everyday life of Africans, the epidemiological and ecological vulnerability of their continent, and West Africa's 'burgeoning metropolis' – the joining-up of a dotted line of cities running along the 'entire stretch of coast from Abidjan eastward to Lagos' to form a single, immense conurbation.

Kaplan was terrified by the rising demographic pressure on the poorest continent. Transfixed by the multiplicity of impending threats 'out of Africa', he failed to pay sufficient attention to the continent's intergenerational divide and its battle over female empowerment. He ignored half of Africa – its hundreds of millions of girls and women. He saw only 'hordes' of young men whom he likened to 'loose molecules in a very unstable social fluid, a fluid that was clearly on the verge of igniting'. He jumped to the conclusion that these youngsters would submerge the old father figures, while in fact their victory was, and still is, hard to imagine in an Africa that remains in large measure gerontocratic. Only some among the many will enjoy the exhilaration and privileges of power. The others, the grand mass of young men and women, have only their numerical strength to count on. As available (and expendable) foot soldiers, they will march behind rebel and opposition leaders or, more often to their advantage, the highest bidders among the established order.

Empty Granaries, Coveted Land

Between 2010 and 2020, some 200 million people will be added to the population of sub-Saharan Africa. This could be good news on a continent whose soil is comparable in quality to that of India – which has attained food self-sufficiency since its Green Revolution in the 1970s – and which includes about 60 per cent of the world's arable land not yet put into production. But in the current state of sub-Saharan Africa, 200 million more inhabitants pose a problem. Leaving aside the effects of global warming, which will further destabilize the fragile ecosystems in the entire Sahel region, some 400 million people already suffer from chronic malnutrition and nearly 100 million pre-school infants are anaemic (Sommers 2015: loc. 1018–23). The growth of 60 per cent of all children is impaired because of inadequate nutrition, with severe consequences for their physical or intellectual development. A Green Revolution in sub-Saharan Africa is sorely needed, but it is not on the horizon. Ninety-six per cent of its peasants cultivate plots of less than 5 hectares, and many refrain from investing in fertilizers and other agricultural inputs as their land titles are frequently in dispute (Brunel 2014: 192). According to the World Bank, cereal yield per hectare south of the Sahara stood at 1.4 tons in 2016 versus 5.7 tons in France, 7 tons in the UK and 8.1 tons in the United States. Farmers obtained less than half a litre of milk per day per cow compared with an average of 25 litres in France, the UK and the United States. And in all three, more than 90 per cent of farmers use tractors compared with just 2 per cent south of the Sahara. In tropical Africa, only 5 per cent of cropland is irrigated compared with 58 per cent in India.

'Accelerated urbanization is more a symptom of agricultural difficulties than a consequence of agrarian modernization', Sylvie Brunel argues (2014: 169). She adds that by 2030, half a billion more Africans will have left the countryside 'to live in cities or, rather, slums'. What will they eat? Relying on international charity would be a deadly wager in a world where nutritional needs are set to increase by 70 per cent between now and 2050, when the world's population is expected to reach 9 billion people. By the middle of this century, Africa will need to have quintupled its agricultural production to guarantee its food security. Otherwise, it will have to import much of its food supply, at high prices. Already, a country like Nigeria spends about 10 billion dollars per year – nearly 40 per cent of its 2016 oil revenues, and around 15 per cent if the price of crude were to rise to its previous highs – to import the foodstuff it does not produce. It ought, at the same time, to be importing machine tools to develop its own industry, modernize smallholder agriculture and eventually create well-paying jobs. 'Soil not oil' (Olopade 2014: 167) should have been the mantra not just for Nigeria, but for every other petroleum-producing country south of the Sahara.

Demographic pressure on natural resources such as arable land and water heightens the risk of conflict. In the Darfur region of western Sudan, an almost seven-fold population increase since independence in 1956 – when the number of inhabitants was 1.3 million compared with more than 9 million in 2017 – is straining an environment already hit hard by desertification. In addition, Darfur is saddled with a difficult historical legacy. This includes the destruction of local land titles – *hakura* – during the Mahdist Revolution at the end of the nineteenth century, the 'native administration' put in place under British colonial rule that exacerbated tensions between sedentary peasants and cattle or camel herders, and the violence meted out since 2003 by tribal militias armed by Sudanese president Omar al-Bashir and known as *janjawid* – 'evil on horseback'. In western Sudan, the stage was set for murderous conflict. That's certainly not the case everywhere in the Sahel. But across the region, demographic stress and, in its wake, ecological degradation and socio-economic hardship are always part of the local mix. Jointly, they also fuel conflict in Mali, Burkina Faso, Niger and Chad.

Thomas Robert Malthus (1766–1834) authored one of the most influential books on demography, *An Essay on the Principle of Population*, which was reprinted five times during his lifetime. At the end of the nineteenth century, one of his biographers called him 'the best-abused man of the age' (Bonar 1885: 2). No doubt, Malthus's unpopularity has something to do with his two dour and unyielding assumptions: that Mother Earth has limited resources and therefore can sustain only so many people, and that human nature is defined by self-interest. But his tarnished reputation is chiefly due to a few lines that he added to the second edition of his book, released in 1803, and then expunged from subsequent reprints to calm the storm of indignation. More than 200 years later, this passage, known to posterity as 'Nature's Feast', has a bleak topicality which makes it worth quoting in full:

> A man who is born into a world already possessed, if he cannot get subsistence from his parents on whom he has a just demand, and if the society do not want his labour, has no claim of right to the smallest portion of food, and, in fact, has no business to be where he is. At nature's mighty feast there is no vacant cover for him. She tells him to be gone, and will quickly execute her own orders, if he does not work upon the compassion of some of her guests. If these guests get up and make room for him, other intruders immediately appear demanding the same favour. The report of a provision for all that come, fills the hall with numerous claimants. The order and harmony of the feast is disturbed, the plenty that before reigned is changed into scarcity; and the happiness of the guests is destroyed by the spectacle of misery and dependence in every part of the hall, and by the clamorous importunity of those, who are justly enraged at not finding the provision which they had been taught to expect.

If the world were indeed, as Malthus posited, a bounded and amoral universe, this would be the fate reserved for the next two or three generations of Africans.

Even in the world as it is – its harshness extenuated by small acts of kindness and, in theory, universal rights – a principle that could be called 'demographic conditionality' is at work. The land dispute in Zimbabwe illustrates how this principle can undergird a conflict. After independence in 1980, Zimbabwe suffered from a flagrant imbalance of land ownership inherited from its Rhodesian past, and stretching back to the colonial 'land grab' at the end of the nineteenth century. Despite the existence of a 'willing buyer-willing seller' land reform programme, white commercial farmers in Zimbabwe – 0.6 per cent of the population – still owned two-thirds of the country's most fertile agricultural land at the beginning of the twenty-first century (Godwin 2006:

58). President Robert Mugabe, revered as the liberator from white domination before his decades in power transformed him into a caricature of the tyrannical 'gerontocrat', couldn't have cared less about agrarian reform in the 1990s: his government earmarked 0.16 per cent of the state budget for its implementation. Only when confronted by a real opposition, the Movement for Democratic Change (MDC), and the unexpected loss in 2000 of a constitutional referendum designed to bolster his own powers, did Mugabe tackle the land issue head on. His 'fast-track land reform' resulted in the invasion and takeover of most white-owned farms by his supporters – who sometimes tormented and killed the owners – and opened the road to his long dictatorship. Despite the violent means employed, many Zimbabweans as well as observers abroad still hoped that the end – 'repossession' as a late response to the colonial land grab – could be good. But such a tit-for-tat reading of the crisis overlooked an important fact: 78 per cent of white-owned farms had been acquired *after* the country's independence, and under strict terms that required the state to renounce its right of first purchase (Godwin 2006: 58).[2] David Stevens was one of these new owners. He had left what was then apartheid South Africa in 1986 to live with his Swedish wife, Maria, and their four children in a country free of *de jure* racial segregation. The first victim of the Mugabe-sanctioned 'repossession' of white-owned land, Stevens died on 1 April 2000 after squatters invaded his farm, forced him to drink diesel oil and, after hours of agony, put a bullet in his head.

Seen through the long lens of history, one can still argue that the seizure of white-owned commercial farms in Zimbabwe did bring about the transfer of economic assets to some 60,000 black peasants now living with their families on land that used to belong to fewer than 2,000 white farmers.[3] The new president, Emmerson Mnangagwa, who with army support forced the nonagenarian Mugabe into retirement in November 2017, has given mixed signals as to whether he intends to reverse the farm invasions which began nearly twenty years ago. But 'fast-track land reform' would not have been as popular in the first place if, in addition to longstanding anti-white rancour that Mugabe could play on, the demographic pressure on land had not driven the president's political survival strategy. At forty-two inhabitants per square kilometre, Zimbabwe is scarcely over-populated. But since Cecil Rhodes and his British South Africa Company, which was granted a Royal Charter in 1889, laid hold of the best lands north of the Limpopo River, the population of what is now Zimbabwe has jumped from 700,000 inhabitants in 1900 to more than 16 million in 2017. If the population of the United Kingdom had grown at the same pace, it would now have more than 900 million inhabitants; they might well be fighting over every square metre of land.

No need to push against open doors. It is evident that in matters of health care, education, employment, housing and the provision of infrastructure and public services, the number of inhabitants splinters the resources of a society that has only just begun to free up the productive capacity of its members. Less obvious are other social and political transformations, inextricably linked to a country's population age structure, and its balanced or unbalanced distribution among different age cohorts. In Africa, especially south of the Sahara, the crucial question today is how the preponderance of young people will affect the very core of societies that have traditionally put a premium on age. What will these societies lose when the elderly, who are more tested in life, are drowned out by a multitude full of energy but lacking experience?

The 'Birth' of Youth

The basic stages of life – infancy, childhood, adulthood, old age – seem like natural biological markers, while marketing creations such as 'teenagers' or 'pre-adolescents' are more easily perceived as artificial. Yet all are constructs linked to particular moments in history and specific conditions of emergence. As the historian Philippe Ariès has shown, the concept of childhood was 'born' in

France in the seventeenth century, when the fertility rate dropped for the first time, and the country saw the beginnings of rudimentary birth control (Ariès 1960). Both phenomena served to deepen the emotional attachment between parents and their children. In turn, the concept of youth was 'born' during the time of the Industrial Revolution, when the division of labour became vastly more specialized. Mimesis – the education of the young to replicate the ways of the elders – was no longer sufficient. A new stage of life was invoked to fill the widening gap between childhood and adulthood. Youth were 'set aside' to prepare for a professional life in a world of work involving ever more fragmented tasks and requiring ever more specialized skill sets. Parents started to send their children away from the family home to a life in the institutions – schools, workshops, universities – where they spent their 'formative years' under the authority of professional instructors. Nowadays the period in which a rising generation is 'in a state of becoming rather than being' is publicly funded in many countries. In others the cost is borne by the family.

In Africa, before the colonial era, 'youth' did not exist in the extensive sense that we understand today. Of course, there were young people and benchmark indices for recorded lifetimes: number of years (often imprecise), number of harvests brought in (more precise). Many precolonial societies in sub-Saharan Africa had complex organizational structures based on age. But for all that, the notion of 'youth' enjoyed no more currency than the intricate division of labour which, in Europe, had given rise to an age group suspended between childhood and adulthood, physically developed but socially still immature.

Initiation and other rites of passage have long determined one's social status in life. That remains true today, and outside of Africa as well. An unmarried mother of sixteen taking care of her child is generally considered more 'adult' than other girls of her age, or a father of the same age who runs away from his responsibilities. Eternal students, living off their parents and sometimes under their roof, are considered 'younger' than workers of the same age already striking out on their own and earning a living. Everywhere – including Africa – youth and other age-based categories are never a purely biological marker. They are social indicators.

Take the example of two African heads of state – Jomo Kenyatta, the father of Kenyan independence, and Yoweri Museveni, the president of Uganda since 1986 – whose lives allow us to track what it meant to be 'young' across sub-Saharan generations since the end of the nineteenth century. Both Kenyatta and Museveni have written on the subject. Kenyatta did so in his book, *Facing Mount Kenya*, published in 1938 as an expansion of his doctoral thesis in anthropology from the London School of Economics; and Museveni in his autobiography, *Sowing the Mustard Seed: The Struggle for Freedom and Democracy in Uganda*, which appeared in 1997.

Kenyatta emerges as a dyed-in-the-wool Kikuyu – Kenya's majority ethnic group – with a strong sense of belonging. He was born 'around 1890', a time when exact birth dates were not yet a concern in much of sub-Saharan Africa. His parents were sedentary farmers, with enough sheep and goats for his father to support several wives, each housed in her proper hut or *nyomba*. 'The homestead is the school', Kenyatta writes, the crucible where the younger generation assimilates the community's scale of values. 'Children do most things in imitation of their elders', an idea that goes beyond individual parenthood and makes each adult an educator and potential mentor. More important perhaps, 'family consists of all members both living and dead'. Education prioritizes 'personal relationships' and the proper code of conduct – the command of repertoire – over learning about 'natural phenomena'. It is 'a rehearsal prior to the performance of the activities which are the serious business of all the members of the tribe'. The main objective is 'the building of character and not the mere acquisition of knowledge . . . Character is formed primarily through relations with other people, and there is really no other way in which it can grow. Europeans assume that, given the right knowledge and ideas, personal relations can be left largely to take care of themselves, and this is perhaps the most fundamental difference in outlook between Africans and Europeans'. Individual identity is secondary to collective identity, and as a consequence, the demands of the group take precedence over any others. Emulation among the young is strongly encouraged but always with a view to enhancing the community's potential. For example, to test the memory of young boys and future herders, cattle from different homesteads are intermingled; the ability to recognize one's own livestock, animal by animal, confers early distinction while failure attracts opprobrium.

Customary education among the Kikuyu constantly evolved and adapted to the demands of the day. However, at least from an outsider's point of view, it didn't overcome contradictory impulses and tensions. For example, adolescent girls were allowed a great deal of sexual freedom, which was encouraged as an enjoyable pastime, while genital mutilation and, later on, a strict submission to the will of the husband were imposed as a cast-iron rule. To mark the passage of young men to the status of 'warrior', their earlobes were pierced. In colonial times, this was done between eighteen and twenty years of age. But by the time Kenyatta became president in 1964, the age bracket had slipped to between twelve and sixteen years old. What did not change, however, was the principle that education is everyone's business, from the village to the entire ethnic community. 'In a European's life', Kenyatta wrote, 'the school is usually the first big influence which takes the child away from its parents and brings it as an individual into a separate relationship with the State, but Kikuyu boys and girls do not have to make this break'. That is not to say that they must remain confined to their culture. When he was almost twenty, Kenyatta left his village to study at a Christian missionary school where he was baptized Johnstone Kamau. He went on to live in London and briefly in Moscow. Kenyatta wrote his dissertation in London under the supervision of Bronislaw Malinowski, one of the most eminent anthropologists of the twentieth century. He did not return to Kenya until fifteen years later, shortly after the end of the Second World War, when he took part in the burgeoning anti-colonial struggle. Accused – possibly wrongly – of being a leader in the Mau Mau rebellion, he spent eight years in prison before being released in 1961. Two years later, he led his country to independence.

Yoweri Kaguta Museveni was born in the southwest of Uganda 'around 1944', a half century after Kenyatta. At first glance, his childhood seems as traditional as the Kenyan leader's. In accordance with Bahima custom, his parents, who were cattle herders, set him to work on the chores that fell to the youngest son; Museveni cleaned the manure from the family's cattle pen with his hands at the age of four. When he was not much older, he was heaved astride the back of a cow, assegai – a light spear – in hand. 'This is your cow, protect it!', he was told: the order was a test of courage at the heart of his initiation. Up to that age, he spoke only his tribal language, Runyankole. His early education was focused almost exclusively on 'character formation'.

A closer look reveals that the imprecision surrounding Museveni's date of birth was probably an attempt at dissimulation: having become president, Museveni tried to undercut the constitutional age limit to run again for office. More importantly, as he explains in his autobiography, by the time of his childhood 'the clan system had largely broken down'. Children had started going to state school, where they were taught in English. Their instruction largely exceeded, and subsumed, what they learned at home with their parents. At least as consequential was the impact that the adoption of Christianity had on the life of Museveni's family. Though the father remained polygamous, the embrace of a new faith changed much of their daily routine, including their eating habits. Until then, they had lived on milk and meat. Now they 'took the revolutionary step of eating non-milk foods like beans, sweet potatoes and groundnuts for the first time . . . "Christianisation" involved an element of modernisation'. At seventeen, Museveni became an evangelical. Born-again Christianity, with its emphasis on 'personal discipline' and renewal, was 'the moral teaching which appealed to me – the idea that you should not squander your life'.

From Kenyatta to Museveni, what it meant to be young had changed over time in an Africa that itself had changed profoundly. In the middle of the 1960s, in the heyday of independence, 'you could deposit your savings at a post office in Uganda and withdraw the money in Dar es Salaam', Museveni remembers. He sent his money ahead when he enrolled in the most progressive university in East Africa, the University of Dar es Salaam, where Walter Rodney – author, a few years later, of *How Europe Underdeveloped Africa* – was teaching, among other radical trailblazers. Museveni rubbed shoulders with John Garang, the budding leader of the South Sudanese rebellion, and Stokely Carmichael, the American civil rights leader who had fallen out with his fellow Black Panthers and 'returned' to Mother Africa. When Tanzanian president Julius Nyerere came to the campus and addressed the students, but then refused to engage in a dialogue with them, Museveni turned on the father of African socialism – *ujamaa* or 'extended family' in Swahili – and accused him, among other things, of 'painting a false image of an ideal African society which was messed up by the Europeans'. Regarding Europeans, Museveni had by then already made up his mind: 'Whites are not genuine.'

One would be as guilty of the same sort of sweeping generalization if one thought that the accounts of two young East Africans allowed us to grasp what 'being young' meant south of the Sahara between the end of the nineteenth and the middle of the twentieth century. But, sketchy as they are, the impressions we glean from their life stories tell us right away that Kenyatta would never have written the sentences that figure in Museveni's autobiography. While Kenyatta wrote a rigorous yet sympathetic anthropological study – prefaced by Malinowski – about his own ethnic group, Museveni looked at his countrymen from a remove, and identified unfinished business: an 'incomplete social metamorphosis'. He concluded: 'I realized that my people were badly off, and I decided to educate them.' As I write these lines, Museveni's mission has been going on for more than thirty years. And what began as education has ended in autocracy.[4]

Suicides in a Blue Frock Coat

As an archaeologist of knowledge, Michel Foucault has ironically spoken of the 'Euro-construction of youth'. But this new stage of life, though it was 'born' on the Old Continent, has become globalized and now encompasses very disparate realities, including the singularly overprotective parenting style of the American middle class (assuming this vast socio-economic category still means any one thing). The idea of 'youth' circulates around the globe and has been adopted in places where its conditions of emergence have never occurred. That it is a winning proposition for any society to defer the social responsibility of its rising generation, so that adolescents can learn more now and better produce in the long run, is today a credo shared worldwide. The dissemination of this belief has been subsidized by the First World with amounts of aid – public and private funds for 'youth projects' – that surpass by far what Third World governments could possibly spend on their youth cohorts. Nowhere is this truer than south of the Sahara. As a result, the youth concept is as operative today in sub-Saharan Africa as it is, let's say, in the United States. But, like the middle-class category in America, the youth category south of the Sahara has grown too capacious to denote anything in particular any longer: when roughly 80 per cent of the population is less than thirty years old, 'youth' is as blurry and out of focus as the middle class in the United States.

The two groups are worth a quick look. The American middle class is hegemonic, but only because it is defined – actually, ill-defined – by an annual income of anywhere from 30,000 to 350,000 US dollars, a range that excludes just the top 2 per cent and the bottom 10 per cent, the ultra-wealthy nabobs and the impoverished wretches. Using this massive income bracket,

which comprises 88 per cent of the population, masks the growing inequality among the vast majority of Americans. By the same
token, 'defining' African youth on the basis of an age bracket
that comprises 80 per cent of the population, and an even higher
percentage of city dwellers, misses the point. Although youth
is linked to biological age, it is essentially a social characteriza-
tion and, as such, depends on the context that varies so greatly
through time and space. An age bracket is never enough for us
to understand what youth *means* at a certain historical moment
or in a given place. Just because an American, a Japanese and a
Nigerian are each twenty years old does not mean that 'being
twenty' is the same in New York, Tokyo and Lagos. For the same
reason, to be young in the Germany of Angela Merkel has little in
common with being young in the German *Kulturnation* – before
the country was unified politically – towards the end of the eighteenth century, when a precocious genius, Johann Wolfgang von
Goethe, joined the *Sturm und Drang*, an emotional outburst in
German literature and music best rendered as 'storm and drive'.
At the age of twenty-four, Goethe published the loosely autobiographical novel *The Sorrows of Young Werther*, a story of tragic,
unrequited love. It made him a celebrity overnight, and it spread
the so-called 'Werther fever' throughout Europe. Forlorn young
lovers, sporting blue frock coats and yellow vests, like Werther,
and with a copy of the bestseller slipped inside their pocket, ended
their lives in the first modern example of copycat suicide.

In his 1992 study, 'The Youth Union of Thiès', a Senegalese
city about 70 kilometres east of Dakar, the late French historian,
Jean Suret-Canale, noted that

> the term 'youth organisation' can be misleading for a European
> reader, for whom 'young' generally refers to people under the
> age of twenty-five (between eighteen and twenty-five, roughly)
> and, at a push, under the age of thirty. But in Africa, and pretty
> much all societies organized by age groups, the term 'youth' is
> generally used in contrast to the 'elders' who, due to their age,

hold authority. 'Youth' refers to men in the prime of their life (who, in the past, fought the wars); understood this way, the category extends until forty years old, or even beyond. (Suret-Canale in D'Almeida-Topor et al. 1992: 46)

In other words, youth marks a social status more than a biological age. To account for this traditional perception, but also to deal with the contemporary challenges for young Africans in 'achieving' adulthood, the Pan-African political organization the African Union (AU) has set the upper limit of its definition of youth at thirty-five years old – a fact that often strikes outsiders to the continent as odd.

This comparative conundrum has no solution. While the meaning of 'youth' changes across time and space, the common denominator identifying young people from different eras or countries – a fixed age bracket – is not only arbitrary but devoid of any societal meaning. Of course, in response to the question 'what does it mean to be young?' at any particular time or place, the answer 'it means to be between eighteen and twenty-five years of age' falls risibly short. But for broad comparative studies, it's the only answer there is.

Brothers and Sisters in Faith

Along with the revolution in everyday life wrought by the spread of the mobile telephone, the most profound change in contemporary Africa is the religious renewal among Christians and Muslims. This also greatly matters to the rest of the world since sub-Saharan Africa – a spiritual seedbed with record growth rates – will determine the future of these two great monotheistic religions. In 2015, 16 per cent of Muslims and 26 per cent of Christians worldwide lived south of the Sahara. By 2060, those figures will rise to 27 per cent of the world's Muslims, and 42 per cent of the world's Christian population – globally, four out of every ten followers of Jesus Christ.

If a newfound faith is the answer, what was the question?[5] On the Christian side, the spiritual renewal is primarily evangelical, from self-proclaimed prophets in shanty towns to worldwide federations of born-again believers. This efflorescence of Protestant cults, which began some forty years ago, promises 'healing', if not outright 'miracles', but also dispenses aid in lieu of the failing state – medical care, education, social security writ large. Its participatory religious services provide transcendental moments often subsumed under the heading 'charismatic revolution'. At an individual and experiential level, 'rupture by rapture' sums up the synergy these cults achieve by combining an alternative spirituality with spectacular, often ecstatic performances. On the Muslim side, there is still no generic term for these reshaped expressions of faith that are more and more evident in African daily life. They are often Salafist, the school of Sunni Islam that builds on 'tradition' – *sunni* – and the precedent set by the pious 'forebears' – *salaf* – to condemn theological innovation and to advocate literal adherence to Islamic law. The media rarely miss out on an opportunity to call Salafism 'radical' in its opposition to 'Western rationality'. This tends to obfuscate the fact that Pentecostalism and other evangelical denominations are hardly less virulent and irrational. Admittedly, holy wars fought for the advent of millenarian rule – the predicted thousand-year-long Kingdom of God on Earth after the Second Coming of Jesus Christ – are unheard of these days; but Christian Pied Pipers hoping to lure to their temples a flock of youthful believers are not. Paul Gifford touches on just this point when he calls these new evangelical temples 'youth churches' (Gifford 1998: 88, 89; cf. Spinks 2002: 195). Under their influence, the two disempowered majorities south of the Sahara – women and young people – are checking out of the polity, figuratively if not literally, to reinvent themselves in spiritual life or abroad, in the diaspora.

Since the late 1970s, evangelical beliefs have been a ferment of change more consequential than the conquest of power and the command of the state apparatus could ever have been.

'Born-again' Africa is the wholesale negation of traditional Africa. The 'Gospel of prosperity' – the blessing of material wealth and, in particular, of money as the coinage of happiness – upends the rules of reciprocity and substitutes frayed kinship ties with the newfound, sturdy solidarity among 'brothers and sisters in faith'. With their help and God as an all-mighty ally, born-again Africans – more individualistic than their parents but less isolated than their counterparts in the West – prove resistant to the pressures of the extended family; and this at the very moment when large numbers of poor young people hollow out traditional obligations of sharing, the so-called 'rendezvous of give and take'. To pick an example from everyday life, involving one of the most elementary rules of traditional sociability: when a relative visits, they are automatically offered a seat at the dinner table. But that rule is far harder to respect when the dining room is transformed into a refectory by a swarm of 'cousins', none of whom is capable of returning the favour and responding in kind. Respecting etiquette here would lead to the financial ruin of those who are still just getting by. The evangelical home, today more often than not a nuclear family, will refuse such rules, and at times not hesitate to show cousins the door, even, perhaps, lecturing them on the need to please God by 'succeeding in life' instead of 'sponging off'.

Nicolas Argenti highlights the 'Pentecostal rejection of everything the elders stood for' and adds that Pentecostalism 'focuses on achieving a continuous state of rupture with the past by means of continuous personal renewal, and thereby to establish a life of freedom from enslavement by Satan – where Satan can be seen as an embodiment of the gerontocratic structures that so alienate the young' (2002: 141). The charismatic revolution thus has tended to eliminate age and the masculine gender as *the* criteria for admission to society's most sought-after positions. Wisdom, the harvest reaped from life experience, is no longer extolled; it is now relegated to the back pews by the more utilitarian knowledge that comes from young digital natives and their expertise with computers, the internet, mobile phones. The role and status of young women in particular has radically changed, but they are not alone in discovering that this emancipation comes at a price. Subaltern groups have been liberated and, at the same time, subjected to new strictures and restrictions, as the born-again existence is predicated on personal responsibility and a regimen of invasive rules that brook neither excuses nor exceptions – no more 'African time', bawdy words, or being 'three sheets to the wind'; no more debauchery *tout court*; instead, it's the alarm clock, or even an Apple Watch, discipline and decency in all circumstances, and a new Protestant ethic. The only 'spirits' to be indulged in are those of the holy variety, or of capitalism. There is still dancing in the heart of the born-again African, but the reformed subject is no longer a party to endless feasts, animal sacrifices, fetish cults and visits to the Sacred Grove. In their new lifestyle, evangelicals challenge so-called 'African' traditions, including the customary recriminations against their former colonizer, as so many roadblocks on the path to progress. All of this makes the charismatic revolution a sort of civilizing mission of divine inspiration led by the young.

Of course, a youth revolt galvanized by religion is hardly a new phenomenon. On the Muslim side, Murray Last (2005) has put in perspective intergenerational contestation in northern Nigeria since the beginning of the late eighteenth century. He points out that over that period, youth – *dattijai* – inspired by their faith have four times upended the established order of the elders – *yara*. First, when they turned themselves into swords of the Koran in a jihad from 1804 to 1808 that led to the establishment of the Caliphate of Sokoto; then, between 1900 and 1910, in the face of British colonial dominance and the 'sell-out' of their elders; next, during the 1950s, and the struggle for independence that was at the heart of every political party, the new conduit of mass mobilization; and finally, since the second half of the 1990s, by promoting *sharia*, literally the 'right path leading to a water hole in the desert'. For many young Muslims in Nigeria, Koranic law has become the last bulwark against Western corruption.

Since 2000, the twelve northern states of the Nigerian federation have applied *sharia* alongside the common law inherited
from their British colonizer. Removed from its local context,
the popularity of Koranic law and the enemies of the West –
yesterday Osama bin Laden, today the Islamic State (ISIS) and
Boko Haram, whose name translates from the Hausa as 'Western
education is forbidden' for Muslims – may seem very hard to
understand. From the outside, however, it is equally difficult to
imagine what daily life resembles when everything can be bought
and sold, from a construction permit to an educational diploma,
the probity of a civil servant or the virtue of a young woman; or
when local elected officials meet just once a year, on the day of the
federal allocation that is supposed to fund a year's worth of activities but disappears into their pockets; or when, at the request of a
'big man', security forces go in and raze a neighbourhood, blindly
shooting and killing to punish those deemed 'complicit' with a
political rival for having voted for him. Or, indeed, when the
West seems to trample on the rest. In these circumstances, where
personal integrity is denied to the weakest, they wish for nothing better – as did the Swiss-born writer and adventurer Isabelle
Eberhardt, alias Si Mahmoud Saadi – than to take refuge *In the
Warm Shadow of Islam*.[6]

The world of adults often seems eminently blameworthy to
young people. However, Murray Last stresses that the four 'power
inversions' in northern Nigeria have paradoxically rendered more
permeable the supposedly solid demarcation between young and
old; so much so that he wonders whether the young are truly
trying to supplant the elders, or merely to stop them from carrying on politics as usual and, in the end, to share with them a new
way of running the country. That was, after all, also the original
intention of al-Shabaab – 'youth' in Arabic – the youth wing of
the Islamic Courts Union (ICU), which had been in power in
Somalia in 2006 when Ethiopia invaded their country with the
consent, if not at the instigation, of the United States. Al-Shabaab
took the lead in the national resistance to foreign interference,

thus inheriting the mantle of the Somalia Youth League, the country's first political party, founded in 1948 and aimed at bringing about a unified and independent Somalia, a goal achieved in 1960. Outside of any religious context, this is reminiscent of the gauntlet thrown down by Nelson Mandela, then the leader of the African National Congress's Youth League, to radicalize the fight against racial discrimination in South Africa. Mandela launched the armed struggle on 16 December 1961 – the day after ANC president Albert Luthuli was awarded the Nobel Peace Prize – in order to force the hand of the anti-apartheid movement's ageing leaders, who were 'too Gandhian' for his taste.[7]

Democracy, a Barmecide Feast

In 2003, Richard Cincotta, Robert Engelman and Daniele Anastasion – a demographer, a former journalist who had founded a research group on population and the environment, and a documentary filmmaker with an interest in Africa – made a seminal contribution to the refoundation of demography. Entitled *The Security Demographic: Population and Civil Conflict After the Cold War*, their study was relatively concise, about a hundred pages of text with numerous graphs and statistics. It looked at the 1990s, the first decade after the end of the Cold War, and included a large sampling of countries, not just in Africa. The authors assessed four variables and their correlation with outbreaks of collective violence, in most cases civil war: a population with a 'youth bulge', technically a society where 40 per cent of the population between fifteen and sixty-four is younger than thirty; an urban growth rate above 3 per cent a year; high HIV/AIDS prevalence; and, finally, a scarcity of cropland and water. Among these factors, the presence of a large number of young people – the 'security demographic' referenced in the title – turned out to be by far the most important. In the 1990s, a 'youth bulge' more than doubled the likelihood that a country would experience a civil war. The correlation with a scarcity of cropland and water was less significant but, as we have seen in Zimbabwe, might well have gained importance in Africa since the 1990s, due to the fast increasing demographic pressure on natural resources. The two remaining variables, rapid urbanization and HIV/AIDS prevalence, are in fact indirect measures of a population's youthful age structure – it is mostly young people who leave their villages for the city and, being sexually more active than other age groups, are more likely to become infected with HIV/AIDS.

Is a sizeable youth cohort then responsible for the outbreak of collective violence? Yes and no. Yes, since the study supports the idea that, all other things being equal, a very large number of young people, and in particular young men, increases the risk of internal strife. No, because these young people are not intrinsically bellicose, but react to the conditions of their life – access to education, employment, health, their status in the social hierarchy – which enrage them all the more as they are beyond their control. These conditions depend on their country's quality of governance. Either way, we rediscover what any insurance agent would have been able to tell us from experience: the vast majority of traffic accidents are not caused by elderly women but by young men, while not all young men act out at the steering wheel and end up in traffic accidents.

The Security Demographic was the first of three publications in a ten-year span that reclaimed centre stage for demography among the social sciences. The other two were *The Shape of Things to Come: Why Age Structure Matters to a Safer, More Equitable World* (Leahy et al. 2007), and the edited volume *Political Demography: How Population Changes Are Reshaping International Security and National Politics* (Goldstone et al. 2011). All three moved the debate beyond the hypnotic obsession with a 'demographic explosion' and the problems it posed for feeding an increasingly 'overpopulated' world. It was time to turn the page. Since the publication of the 1968 bestseller by Paul Ehrlich, *The Population Bomb*, demography had been confined to a narrow role as the panicked guardian of the planet's resources. By 1980, that message was relayed by the North-South Commission whose report, written under the chairmanship of former West German chancellor Willy Brandt, was subtitled 'A Program for Survival'. It reprised the familiar trope, but this time repainted in the Third World colours of the day. Since then, as the perils of climate change have become more and more evident, the current political ecology has reformulated the same essential message but with new language.

The 'demographic profile' or age structure of a population – that is, not only its numerical significance and growth rate but also the relative weights of its different age cohorts and the dynamics among them – provide insights and data as fundamental to a society as its socio-economic parameters. But many of us accept much more willingly the idea that it is economic fundamentals that determine our collective destiny rather than demography. Wrongly, I think, since the material production of a community hinges on its biological reproduction. There is no reason to believe on the one hand that the economy defines the political latitude of a community and, on the other, to be annoyed at the sway demographics holds over a country's future. Neither one nor the other settles societal matters in any deterministic, pre-ordained way. One of the fathers of modern sociology, Auguste Comte, is often quoted as having said: 'Demography is destiny.' But human destiny is not causality, the succession of cause and effect *no matter what*. Rather, it is chance brought to life by continuous choice. Under certain demographic conditions, certain outcomes are *more likely* than others – but we can tip the balance.

With this in mind, Africa's exceptionally young demographic profile lessens the chances of sustainable democracy, especially south of the Sahara. Every study confirms this negative correlation. That said, the few studies comparing political instability in mountainous versus flat countries also attest to the more 'rebellious' character of rugged terrain ... Correlation is not reason, even though in this instance political scientists confirm the democratic fragility of 'youth bulge' countries. Paul Collier summarizes their research: 'in low-income societies democracy is

dangerous, and in high-income societies dictatorship is dangerous' (2009: 132). In both cases, but for opposite reasons, instability
threatens the system. In low-income countries, the ability to cry
out for more can lead to an explosion inasmuch as the resources to
satisfy those demands do not exist; in high-income countries with
an autocratic government, the repression of the right to speak
freely is implosive.

How can we explain Africa's 'democratic handicap', especially
south of the Sahara? To start with, it is necessary to clarify an
important point: the argument is not about the *advent* of democracy but rather about its *sustainability*. Democracy is already 'out
there', available to any population that wishes for the government of the people – in much the same way that the concept
of 'youth' has been globalized and is now available worldwide,
including in sub-Saharan Africa where the historical conditions
of emergence have not materialized. Yet it is not enough simply
to desire to create the conditions necessary for democracy to take
root and thrive. After the collapse of the Soviet bloc, the African
henchmen of the Cold War were toppled by 'the wind blowing
from the east' – a reference to the pro-democracy push in sub-
Saharan Africa and a reminder of British Prime Minister Harold
Macmillan's famous 'wind of change' speech in 1960, at the dawn
of African independence. But forty years later, and despite the
democratic re-ignition that the Arab Spring could have sparked in
2011, the state of democracy in Africa is weak. North and south
of the Sahara, the people's sovereignty resembles the Barmecide
feast in *The Arabian Nights*: only an appearance of abundance and
nothing else. In reality, the table is empty and the Barmecide
prince laughs at his poor guest, Schacabac. Terrified, the beggar
plays along, until forced to drink the host's 'excellent wine', at
which point he snaps and pummels his host under the pretext of
being drunk . . .

One explanation of the fragility of African democracies is the
inherent instability of societies that are unable to respond to the
basic needs of their people – in Africa, their mostly young people

– and their aspiration to build lives of their own. Thomas Hobbes wrote in *Leviathan* that the purpose of the State is to rescue its people from the state of nature, 'the war of all against all'. If so, it is in the self-interest of the 'haves' in Africa to support with all their resources possible an authoritarian regime – even at the expense of curtailing their own liberty – in order to keep the desperate masses in check. A second explanation for the brittleness of democracy in Africa can be found in Charles Tilly's reflections on democracy (2007: 13–15). The American social scientist notes that democracy takes root where 'political relations between the state and its citizens feature broad, equal, protected and mutually binding consultation'. But the 'categorical inequality' that age still constitutes in Africa – where the primacy of the elders effectively reduces the young, and in particular young women, to second-tier citizens – stands in the way of equal and unhindered access to the state. The 'principle of seniority' is a significant obstacle to democracy, in much the same way that the disenfranchisement of women at one time weakened Western countries. To overcome this handicap, Africa's second-class citizens will need to be fully emancipated. But that battle is far from being won. Under current conditions, the likelihood that Africa's frustrated youth will fill the ranks of armed 'anti-system' groups is as high as the chance that the 'social cadets' of the continent will achieve true democratization by peaceful means.

Former French president Jacques Chirac argued in February 1990 that 'Africa is lacking the maturity for multiparty politics.'[8] Just months after the fall of the Berlin Wall, at the very moment when crowds were demonstrating in sub-Saharan capitals against the single-party states that had prevailed throughout the Cold War period, and for the right to partake in free and fair elections, Chirac was excoriated. I think for three eminently good reasons. First, because his principal argument – 'the risk of ethnic rivalry' – doesn't hold water. If it were admissible, then the existence of any cleavage, from different social classes to different religious communities, would make going to the polls too dangerous in most countries – and there would be no democracy anywhere. Secondly, Chirac was wrong because, as Aristotle observed in his *Nicomachean Ethics*, one learns how to play the harp by playing the harp, and not by waiting until one is 'mature' enough to master the instrument. Finally, Chirac was wrong because, as we have already made clear, democracy no longer has to be invented, it already exists and every nation in the world is free to choose it. However, the former president did make a valid point, even though it was lost in his condescending infantilization of Africa: the overwhelming number of young people in contemporary Africa, and their 'categorical inequality', *do* undermine the sustainability of democracy on the continent. The consolidation of democracy will remain a task more arduous than elsewhere for the next two or three generations.

Like the imaginary island of Peter Pan, Africa is a Neverland of young people. When 'the boy who wouldn't grow up' returns to the Darlings' London home to look for the shadow he had left during an earlier visit, he manages to wake up Wendy and her two young brothers. They marvel that he knows how to fly. He tells them to copy him, and the children succeed . . . almost. To fly, you have to do more than believe; you need a bit of magic, in this case, some of Tinker Bell's fairy dust. And voilà, they all fly away to Neverland, which turns out to be a real nightmare. Not only is there the frightful Captain Hook, his gang of pirates, a sinister crocodile, American Indians, and no girls at all before the arrival of Wendy. There is also the 'rule' that death will strike any boy who becomes an adult – Peter Pan takes care of that. He is joyous, innocent and heartless; that is to say, he makes no distinction between reality and play, and he has no memories because they will force him to grow up. And he is all the prouder of himself because he has no past, it's been forgotten, and no future, because he refuses to grow up. Peter Pan lives in the eternal present, perpetually 'in the state of becoming rather than being'. Hundreds of millions of young Africans face a similar dilemma.

3

Emerging Africa

In Africa south of the Sahara, skyscrapers coexist with mud huts, bush taxis with Uber, and 4G mobile networks with 'talking drums'; in business, sport and entrance exams, merit-based competition often includes 'sacrifices' in addition to hard work and learning. 'All time is eternally present', wrote T. S. Eliot in his poem *Four Quartets*, published in 1943.

As the Second World War drew to a close, a German-Jewish philosopher and refugee to the United States, Ernst Bloch, was working in the Princeton University library on his magnum opus. He wanted to call it *Dreams of a Better World*. But the book was published in the mid-1950s under the title *The Principle of Hope*. In this long reflection on time and the utopias that mankind had devised to make it more hospitable, Bloch proposed *die Gleichzeitigkeit des Ungleichzeitigen*, which is almost untranslatable, but means something like: 'the simultaneity of epochs that elsewhere have been successive'. Far more than a simple compression of historical periods, this concept calls for an end to the idea of orthogenesis – the notion that development always passes through various points of progress or 'stages'[1] (a notion that underpins all 'civilizing missions', from colonization to present-day NGOs). Africa is underdeveloped, certainly and by all measurable standards; yet, seeing it through Bloch's eyes, we understand why it is not 'backward'. Rather it is somewhere else, a place no other part of the world has ever been to, precisely because of the singular coexistence in Africa of what would be 'old' and 'new' in Europe and America. Nowhere else in the world apart from Africa south of the Sahara is time telescoped with such contrasting violence, sometimes creative, sometimes destructive, but always in the likeness of Africa's multitude of young people, who are both the vanguard of progress and its vandals, both makers and breakers.

In today's Africa, one can be born in Nioro, deep in the Sahel, and become an astrophysicist at NASA, then the prime minister of Mali, and later president of Microsoft Africa. But for every Modibo Diarra, how many nameless Africans die in their infancy? How many go to a school – assuming they, and especially girls, attend one at all – that will prepare them to compete in the world? How many enter the workforce with a chance of finding remunerative employment? How many will become old without becoming adults, without the means to leave their parents' home, set up their own household and live the life of their choice? Africa, the island-continent of youth, is also the 'lost land' of failed adulthood where hundreds of millions of castaways are waiting for a life of fulfilment beyond their reach.

The tension between the exception and the rule is strong in Africa, where epochs that elsewhere have been successive co-inhabit the here and now, and where the present often jars with what the continent has the potential to become in the future. Through the scrim of conflicting temporalities, the real and the virtual constantly need to be reconciled. For some, including myself, Africa comes out of this thought process as 'a place in the world' like any other (Ferguson 2006: 1–25), certainly with its own history but without any *essential* difference that could be ascribed to 'Africanness'. It is a place where standard benchmarks apply and universal aspirations are shared – something

Africans confirm every day when they leave their continent for a better life elsewhere. But for others, 'Africanness' is more than just a geographical reference. For them, Africa is an extraordinary continent, either *sui generis* – often a byword for 'exotic' – or a mere fantasy, an 'invention' of the West à la Edward Said. The Palestinian-born scholar of postcolonialism argued that the Orient only existed in the eyes of the Western Orientalist.[2] By the same token, 'Africanness' only exists in the 'colonial library' as a figment of the imagination of Western scholars and adventurers, who found in Africa the West's ultimate foil – the continent of unbridgeable otherness, the shadow that brings Europe to light. African scholars, for their part, have both contradicted and emulated their Western forerunners. Some have turned the tables, reclaiming and embracing 'Africanness' as their own – luminous and redemptive. In the footsteps of the Senegalese historian Cheikh Anta Diop (1923–86), they have substituted Afrocentrism for Eurocentrism. Dark Africa has become 'the bright continent'.[3]

Like others who have been interested in Africa for much of their lives, I am weary of a dialogue of the deaf between the Afro-optimists and the Afro-pessimists. Tired also of the facile way out of this endless quarrel by admonishing both sides that they should 'simply call it what it is', without any presuppositions – as if this could be brought about by fiat or an act of will. In my view, the problem runs much deeper. The altercation between Afro-optimists and Afro-pessimists is not reducible to the trivial choice between 'a glass half full' and a 'glass half empty'. It is instead marked by a visceral drive that has each side go for the other's jugular. Where does this virulence come from? I believe it reflects the extreme asymmetry of age south of the Sahara. One side sees only the world of a handful of elders, the seat of true power, occult and immutable behind change that is never more than superficial. 'This is Africa' – or simply 'TIA' – is their rallying cry, a phrase as peremptory as it is false. It naively presumes an Eternal Return, an endless recurrence of the status quo as the wheel of history turns. The other side finds in the youthful abundance of Africa a future they want to see happen, cheering it on with Nietzsche's imperative: 'Become what you are!' Both sides, the pessimists as well as the optimists, describe an imaginary Africa, a continent they have transformed into their own theme park: a Ferris wheel for the elderly sitting at the westerly edge of their lives; a discovery trail for the young who, having eyes only for the promise of dawn, believe that the best is still to come.

'The truth is in the eye of the beholder.' Yes, but there is more than just one beholder. Africa's image varies depending on the perspective – Western, Chinese, Arab, . . . – but has the likeness of a real place to the extent that these multiple points of view encounter hard facts which, more or less, resist distortion. Still, the image is always slightly blurred for another reason: Africa changes over time, all the time. Its truth – never objective, always intersubjective – can only be found in the consensus of different ways of 'seeing' the continent. But even then we are only left with a freeze frame while Africa's story unfolds frame by frame like a reel of a film. It is a salutary exercise to compare one view of Africa fifty years *before* independence with another fifty years *after* independence through a pair of films whose narrative frameworks overlap: *Out of Africa*, directed by Sidney Pollack (1985), and *White Material*, directed by Claire Denis (2009). Both movies portray Africa through the eyes of a land-owning European woman who, alone and ultimately unsuccessfully, runs a coffee plantation.

Trade Secrets

'I had a farm in Africa, at the foot of the Ngong Hills', the Danish writer Karen Blixen recalls in the famously lyrical opening line of *Out of Africa*, her autobiographical account of her time in Kenya. The same words begin the film version. Blixen, née Dinesen, wrote in English and, at her publisher's insistence, under the male pen name Isak Dinesen. She lived in Kenya from 1913 to 1931, and published *Out of Africa* six years after her departure from East Africa. The film starred Meryl Streep as Blixen and Robert

Redford in the role of her lover, Denys Finch-Hatton. It garnered six Academy Awards, including best picture and best director, but chose to avoid any mention of what was discomfiting in Blixen's life – drug dependency, the strain and stresses of free love, the eccentricities of the 'Happy Valley set', nostalgia for the aristocratic lifestyle, colonialism as escapism from a Europe perceived as decadent and spent, fey in the archaic sense of 'fated to die soon'. The film instead focuses on the intermittent relationship between Finch-Hatton and Blixen, who later spoke of a 'hopeless love between two parallel lines which stretch out at the same time but can never meet'.

In real life, the polyglot Blixen, home-schooled and essentially a social illiterate, was desperate to escape her early twentieth century life in Rungstedlund, north of Copenhagen. She fell in love with her paternal cousin, the dashing equestrian Hans Blixen-Finecke, with whom she had hoped to run a rubber plantation in Asia. When Hans failed to reciprocate, she instead married his twin brother, Baron Bror Blixen-Finecke, and started a coffee plantation in Kenya. Bror had a title, and Karen the money to purchase a farm of 16 square kilometres in the highlands of the British colony. Some 800 Kikuyus lived on the land and provided the manpower to cultivate and harvest the coffee. The enterprise was doomed from the start. The soil was too acidic, and the high altitude of the Ngong hills did not favour the growth of the fragile berries. But Blixen had to wait five years, until the first harvest, to discover this. And then a fire in their warehouse reduced the dream to ashes.

In the film, Karen Blixen is on her own and knows very little about Africa. Bror honours their marriage contract, but in name only, dignifying her with a title and nothing else – not even his presence. He spends his time big-game hunting (he was, in fact, the best hunting guide of his generation, admired and lauded by everyone, including Ernest Hemingway). Bror also 'catches' Maasai girls as well as syphilis, which he transmits to his wife. Between trips to Denmark seeking a cure for the disease, Karen still manages to run the farm with the help of Farah, her Somali right-hand man, and a white foreman whose expertise is purely technical. Farah knows Kenya intimately, but it is not his home. He maintains an imperturbable sense of superiority over both the Kikuyus and the white settlers. Yet the Danish Baroness and her haughty interpreter, while maintaining a respectful distance, nonetheless develop a strong bond of trust. In all of her affairs, romantic and business, Karen wants to improve what she owns, enhance the value of her property. She never views her pursuit of 'progress' as a form of possessiveness. Farah explains to her, among a thousand other things, that the old Kikuyu chief rejects her offer to school his young kinsmen because doing so would undermine his traditional power, which is based on life lessons, and the knowledge that comes with age.

For the first time in a Hollywood movie, Africans, until then always shown as stereotypical 'tribesmen', acquire individual traits. The film, of course, still delivers on Hollywood's staple tropes: Africa, first and foremost, is a luscious setting, an undulating savannah that stretches as far as the eye can see, the kingdom of buffalo, antelope and lion, as well as natives and settlers. Orphans of a 'civilization' that has just witnessed a world war that killed 8.5 million people, Europeans like Blixen want to reconstruct in Kenya a pre-capitalist state. Having turned their back on corrupting materialism, chaotic urban life and a stultifying division of labour, they desire to return to a more 'natural' lifestyle, beginning with working the land and following their own desires. Still, more than anything else, the story's romantic plot dominates the film. Another will-o'-the-wisp of the bush, but even more brilliant and enigmatic than Bror, Denys Finch-Hatton embodies the freedom that has disappeared in more developed countries. He exhibits nonchalance in the face of material worries, a taste for challenge and pleasure. Denys shares himself with Karen, but he belongs exclusively to himself. It is only when Karen has lost her farm, when she has fallen to her knees before the British Governor imploring him to keep the Kikuyus on 'their' land, that Denys returns to her, throwing caution to the wind. In an emptied-out house, the day before Karen's departure, the two lovers dine and dance with a newfound harmony. She tells the African serving them at the table to dispense with the white gloves she hitherto insisted he wear. Denys confesses that his old life, alone but not lonely, is 'ruined' because of her. The next day, after taking off in his Gypsy Moth biplane, he twice circles the landing strip, then plunges to the ground. Denys and his Maasai alter ego, Kamau, are both killed. 'He was not ours, he was not mine', Karen acknowledges, standing in front of his headstone. At the railway station, when she bids farewell to Farah and leaves for Denmark, the Somali for the first time calls her Karen, no longer using 'Msabu', her title as mistress of the house. She offers him her compass. It is the only present Karen had received from Denys, the last possession she can bring herself to let go of.

White Material is a 2010 French movie starring Isabelle Huppert as Maria Vial, a struggling coffee producer with a manic intensity. The film is set in a contemporary African country that is never named but is easily identifiable as the Ivory Coast – a former French colony – during its civil war in the early 2000s. Claire Denis, the director, whom the *New York Times* has acclaimed as 'consistently the most interesting French filmmaker of the twenty-first century', was born in 1946 and grew up in several francophone African countries where her father was a colonial administrator. Denis co-wrote the screenplay with Marie Ndaye, a French novelist whose father is Senegalese. The script depicts Africa as a hostile environment – the blood-red laterite, the pewter-grey sky, the dusty savannah spiked with inselbergs, resonating with deafening noises and utter silences. This is an Africa that rejects 'white material' in the manner of a body rejecting a hostile organism: Europeans, that is to say, and the complicated objects they have introduced on the continent. Like the hot, humid air, the anti-white sentiment in the country is suffocating. When the fighting gets too close, Vial's farmhands all desert her for safer ground. With the harvest set for just a few days later, Vial tries to recruit as many villagers as she can find to take their place. Unknown to her, however, is the fact that André, her ex-husband with the dissipated air that comes from years in the tropics, has already sold the farm to the young and corrupt mayor of the nearby town in exchange for an armed escort out of the war zone. André has taken over the farm from his father, an old man with a cadaverous pallor who haunts the plantation like a spectre: he resembles the divorced couple's only child, Manuel, who is in his early twenties, except that 'Manu' can't even muster the energy to get out of bed in the morning. When Maria blocks the road in a final attempt to stop her plantation workers from leaving, her Burkinabe foreman, Maurice, leading a caravan of departing mopeds, rejects her demand – 'the French army will not come to evacuate *us* by helicopter', he reminds her. Maurice also reproaches her for her obstinacy and her 'failed son'. Cut to the quick, Maria screams at Maurice, though less to hurt him than to vent her pain. 'Manu' is the last man in her life, and Maria is attached to him as she is to 'her' land, but with little grounding in reality in either case.

Although the story takes place over just forty-eight hours, the chronology is confusing, an entanglement of flashbacks. *White Material* opens with fire and plumes of black smoke consuming not only the farm's storage facilities, as in *Out of Africa*, but also 'Manu', who is locked up in the building, still alive but now, after stabbing his grandfather to death, clearly insane. Government forces have set fire to the premises after surprising the rebels in their sleep and slitting their throats – most of them are child soldiers. In the opening scenes we see Maria hurrying across the fields, then clinging to the outside of a crowded bush taxi. Is she really running away? Or will she come back?

Like Africa itself, from Karen Blixen to Maria Vial, whites in Africa have changed – from colonials to expatriates to foreign residents, though they seldom see themselves as immigrants: 'parasites in paradise', as the Kenyan writer Ngugi wa Thiong'o bluntly characterized the Europeans portrayed in *Out of Africa*. In the 1920s, Kenya, one of a handful of so-called 'settlement colonies' in sub-Saharan Africa, had around 2.5 million people and some 40,000 whites, or 1.6 per cent of the population. Today, Kenya has almost 50 million people, and about 70,000 whites, or 0.14 per cent. What is striking is how marginal the numbers of Europeans were and are, more than ever, today. Has the continent finally become the 'Africa of Africans'? The paradox is this: during the course of the last century, which has seen the presence of Europeans go from marginal to insignificant, the other 'white material' – not persons but the objects that represent their modernity – has multiplied and been widely adopted. Whether these are industrial commodities or the new-fangled objects of a twenty-first-century digital lifestyle, what matters is that they are not locally produced. They come from outside, nourishing the 'cargo-cult' of Africa's modernity – the local belief that salvation will arrive in the hold of a ship.

After the era of *Out of Africa*, young Africans began attending colonial schools, and later, schools in their own independent countries. They have persistently chipped away at the power of their elders and replaced their chieftainships by governments based on the bureaucracy of the state. They have become managers of their nation, some shady and disreputable like the mayor in Claire Denis's film; others brilliant and industrious like Modibo Diarra. Who among them are the exceptions that confirm the rule? The dishonest and corrupted or the hard-working and successful? That is the wrong question to ask, all the more so as the two often bleed across any neat distinction. The crucial fact that determines the fate of so many is that Africans are more than ever submerged by 'white material', but still have only limited access to its trade secrets. As long as this situation lasts, modernity to them will remain 'Western', and indeed a white condition.

The 'Gatekeeper State'

The 'failure' of the postcolonial state in Africa is well and widely understood, perhaps too well. But the blinding evidence in many countries of inefficient governance and weak fiscal pressure, where public goods are rare and infrastructure is absent, only teaches us what the postcolonial state is *not*, without telling us anything about what it actually *is* and why it has been able to last until now. Sixty years after independence, it is the African state's staying power that is intriguing. Its 'lack of institutional capacity', in World Bank parlance, resembles apophatic theology: the Almighty is inaccessible to us, and we can only apprehend His divine attributes negatively, as an intaglio design of 'notness'. Or, as Saint Augustine put it: 'If you do understand, it is not God.'

The colonial state was by definition extrinsic. It originated from the outside and was run by foreigners, whose power resided in the metropole, to which the territory was bound by the 'colonial pact', an exclusive economic contract – 'All for the Metropole' was its slogan. Africa's raw materials, from grain to minerals, were destined for the metropolis. In times of war, massive population transfers of military manpower also occurred. In the eyes of many Africans, this foreignness of the state – its extraneous character – translated into a governance that was arbitrary and alienating. However, for those held in a servile condition in Africa, the advent of colonialism, with its promise – though not always honoured – of putting an end to slavery, was welcome news. To a lesser extent, this was also true for women and youth. For Africa's powerful gerontocracy, 'the era of the Whites became the era of insolence, when "children," "their mouths on fire," came out of their silence' (Argenti 2002: 126, quoting Bayart 1989: 151).

The postcolonial state is not simply the inheritor of European administrative practices. Its birth certificate carries two distinct signatures: from inside the country, the popular desire to run the colonials out and speed up the independent state's development; from outside, acknowledgement and recognition by the international community. This acceptance by the world at large, often through the United Nations, is sometimes termed 'negative sovereignty', as opposed to the actual 'positive' capacity of the state to administer its territory. A colourful piece of bunting, a few rhyming phrases set to music, a few embassies abroad and a national football team have often been enough to constitute a state. In this case, truth really lies in the eye of the beholder. As long as the international community clings to the hope that a central power will be reborn from the ashes of the unitary state of Somalia, which collapsed in 1991, it will refuse to recognize the independence of Somaliland, whose institutional capacity is arguably greater than that of 'official' states like the Central African Republic (CAR). Yet the international community upholds the illusion that the authorities in Bangui exert control over the country's hinterland. Its act of faith keeps CAR's 'Phantom State' alive (International Crisis Group 2007).

The euphoria of independence has long since abated, as has the ability of most sub-Saharan states to hasten the pace of their countries' development. To the advantage of its clientelistic base, the postcolonial state has settled into the role of a collector of customs duties, import and export taxes, and external aid – anything that can be easily pocketed at the border, while the interior of the country is neglected as a tax base, both for political reasons and a lack of institutional capacity. The historian Frederick Cooper has called the postcolonial state in Africa a 'gatekeeper state'. The American anthropologist Rebecca Hardin has added another layer to our understanding of the postcolonial state by drawing on the system of 'concessions' which existed under the Ancien Régime, when the French king used to confer 'rights as specific as the planting or cutting of particular trees by clergy, or the placement of vendor stalls in the gardens of the Palais Royal in Paris, and as extensive as the right to explore and trade products from within entire river basins or within entire colonies as empires expanded' (2011: 116). Hardin defines 'concessions' as formal legal arrangements by which foreign actors are entitled to manage and exploit land or other national resources. The beauty of these arrangements is that they not only satisfy rent-seeking states but, even better, reinforce their sovereign power despite the states' inability to exploit their own resources directly themselves. Hardin speaks of 'concessionary politics', a phrase used to describe states with little institutional capacity that conclude, and regularly renegotiate, such contracts in exchange for a licensing fee and a share of the accrued profit. Low-performance states are able to survive – remarkably well, overall – by selling such concessions to private companies or other states in exchange for rent. The example of oil and mineral companies comes immediately to mind, but there is really no limit to what imaginative governments in Africa can do. In the CAR, for example, customs duties were entrusted to a company founded by a former French mercenary; the revenue was shared between him and the state or, more accurately, the head of state (Smith 2015: 110–12). And it's no exaggeration to say that the CAR's national defence had long been subcontracted to the French before it fell to UN peacekeepers. What is fascinating in this political alchemy is that it transmutes incapacity into profits, or base metal into gold: the less the state can act on its own, the more it has to offer to external partners. They stand in for the state and pay it recognition rights – tribute. All this, of course, does not suffice to make a state, especially when the population is growing as rapidly as it is south of the Sahara. But concessionary politics nourish those in power and allow them to prosper, even in extremely poor states such as the CAR. The only drawback for the ruling elite is the exacerbation of power rivalries, since new contenders are incentivized to compete and, if necessary, fight for control of the state. That is a recipe for permanent instability, and often for civil war.

Among other sovereign functions, the postcolonial state subcontracts its national education. As concessionary logic dictates, the failure of its public schools is not addressed except insofar as it paves the way for a profitable privatization – up to and including the outsourcing of higher education. In the Democratic Republic of the Congo (DRC), 71 per cent of schools are private institutions; in Uganda, out of 5,600 secondary schools, nearly 4,000 are private; in Lagos State in Nigeria, three students out of four are enrolled in private schools; and even in the shanty towns around Nairobi, the Kenyan capital, four out of ten students attend private schools, despite the endemic poverty of the slums. In South Africa, almost a quarter of the schools are not authorized by the state, and thus 'technically illegal' (Olopade 2014: 130). The notion of 'private' includes both church-run schools and 'makeshift schools' that are run by hapless parents, as well as for-profit educational factories. Those who can afford it – and they are usually the same members of the elite who go abroad for their medical care – send their children to university in a Western country. African students are welcome. They are either brilliant and on scholarship or their parents are wealthy enough to pay full tuition – at elite US universities up to 60,000 dollars a year, a handsome sum for the university coffers.

In addition to everything else, the postcolonial state in Africa represents the pursuit of 'gerontocracy' by other means. Nowhere else in the world is the difference between the average age of the governed and of the highest office-holders as great: forty-three years compared with thirty-two in Latin America, thirty in Asia, and sixteen in Europe and North America (Moss and Majerowicz 2012). Of course, there are exceptions. Ellen Johnson Sirleaf was elected and re-elected the president of Liberia in 2005 and 2011, the first woman head of state on the continent. And in the DRC, a whole series of young men have come to power, starting with Patrice Lumumba, who was thirty-five when he became that country's first prime minister, while the man who sent him to his death, Mobutu Sese Seko, also took power at thirty-five; and Joseph Kabila, the current head of state, was only twenty-nine when he became Congo's fourth president in 2001. But that doesn't lay gerontocracy to rest. Johnson Sirleaf was sixty-seven when she took office, and seventy-nine when she left; Mobutu was sixty-six when he was toppled, after thirty-two years in power; and Kabila, the successor of his father, Laurent-Désiré, who was assassinated at sixty-one, seems determined – at the time of writing – to grow old remaining in power, no matter the cost.

'A Billion Good Reasons'

The economic vicissitudes of post-independence Africa amount to a long decade of growth, ending with the 1973 oil crisis, two decades of stagnation until the late 1990s, and then a new boom driven by China's demand for raw materials. In 1997, China was Africa's eighty-third ranking trading partner. But in only fifteen years, China rose to the top spot, overtaking Great Britain, then France, and finally the United States. Africa benefited from rising prices for its raw materials and significant investment in its infrastructure – both largely due to Chinese demand and Beijing's newfound interest in the continent. In addition, according to Serge Michaïlof, Africa reaped the dividends of the painful structural adjustment programmes implemented in the 1980s at the behest of the International Monetary Fund and the World Bank (Michaïlof 2015: 24). Between 2000 and 2010, a number of African countries experienced growth rates averaging more than 5 per cent, which allowed them to make real progress despite their demographics. Five of them – Angola, Ethiopia, Rwanda, Chad and Mozambique – surpassed 7 per cent, the threshold for doubling GDP within a decade. Since then, however, an economic slowdown in China has seriously dented this prosperity and thrown into question the 'Africa Rising' theme. Of the five 'lions on the move', first spotted in a 2010 McKinsey report, only Ethiopia, with more than 100 million inhabitants, is not a paper tiger. The four others have retreated to their lair, gravely wounded. And Ethiopia, like post-genocide Rwanda, started from such a low level – a per capita GDP of some 400 US dollars – that its 'miracle' denotes the first light of prosperity, and not its high noon. The continent's three biggest economies – South Africa, Nigeria and Egypt, which together account for more than half of Africa's total GDP and a good portion of its population – have experienced more modest growth rates, while another demographic heavyweight, the DRC, with its 80 million people, is in permanent crisis. In addition, most African countries have developed as consumer markets rather than sites of production.

Independent Africa's economic ups and downs don't lend themselves to a chiaroscuro juxtaposition of 'Africa Rising' and 'Africa Reeling'. Switching the light on and off doesn't do justice to Africa for at least two reasons: first, it doesn't make much sense to lump together fifty-four singular trajectories to label an entire continent either 'promising' or 'hopeless'; second, if one wishes to assess the continent as a whole, there is in fact nothing new coming out of Africa: since the 1950s, the continent's share of world trade has oscillated between 2 and 3 per cent, and its contribution to worldwide GDP has remained between 1.5 and 2 per cent. Since 1990, when the United Nations Development Programme (UNDP) began publishing its Human Development Report, some forty African countries have always brought up the rear of that list. The top performers among them have invariably been the island state of Mauritius and Botswana, respectively ranked 64th and 108th in 2016. Because of the continent's demographic growth, the percentage of Africans having access to electricity in their homes has shown only a modest increase during that same period, from around 20 per cent to 33 per cent. In absolute figures, Africa remains in a separate category: in 2015, the continent's entire electricity output equalled that of Spain or Argentina, countries of less than 50 million people. Even more striking, 20 million New Yorkers – avid consumers of power in a city that never sleeps – used as much electricity as almost a billion Africans living south of the Sahara.

On the whole, the socio-economic picture of independent Africa comprises fifty-four shades of grey. The continent is still waiting for both its green and its industrial revolution. It has jumped straight to mobile telephony, leapfrogging a hard-wired landline system, but has taken only baby steps on the long road leading from the *use* of modern technologies and the consumption of commodities to their local *production*, including research, development and large-scale manufacture. Given Africa's comparatively low level of educational attainment, it is not likely that the continent will play a major role in the planet's transformation into a cyberspace or a global green economy (although the Congo River basin countries could draw a 'green rent' from properly managing one of the planet's rainforest lungs). In a nutshell, Africa will continue for the foreseeable future to be globalized, rather than play an active role in the globalization process that shrinks the world.

And yet, Africa is emerging! A new land of opportunities is rising out of an ocean of misery. In 2012, Coca-Cola was onto something when it plastered giant billboards across the continent that proclaimed: 'A Billion Reasons to Believe in Africa'. That the number of Africa's inhabitants was invoked in these adverts was no accident. Indeed, it is the scaling up of its population that has allowed Africa to turn a corner: in the early 2000s, 13 per cent of its then 1 billion inhabitants earned between 5 and 20 US dollars a day, and therefore had at least some 'extra' spending money beyond the absolute vital minimum. On a continent that had become a demographic billionaire, this added up to a market of about 130 million consumers, a real economic prize. On the heels of this burgeoning middle class, roughly 200 million other Africans who earn between 2 and 5 dollars a day are about to escape from absolute poverty, pushed out of it by the sheer mass of indigents now on the rise. There is little chance the growing number of Africans who can afford to pay for passage to Europe will wait patiently for their turn at the ticket office of prosperity, especially when the social contract remains freighted with inequity towards young people and women. Other precedents, most notably in the Maghreb, make a different scenario much more likely: once a tipping point is reached, internal migration within the continent will no longer function as an escape valve, and a large number of Africans will begin to push open the doors to the entire world, beginning with Europe.

The middle is hard to find in Africa, the world's poorest continent.[4] One can debate endlessly the pros and cons of calling those Africans just above the subsistence level the continent's middle class. But to my mind, putting them in the same category that is used all over the world, even if Africa's middle class enters this income level under the lowest possible bar, allows for comparisons and serves as a reminder that the middle class is less an income bracket than a social definition on which any form of participatory politics – like democracy – rests. The middle class is that segment of the population with sufficient means to engage in public discourse and the affairs of the community. It also embodies a belief in meritocracy as the governing principle of social mobility. Members of the middle class are not rich and powerful enough to be tempted to abrogate the transparency of the political system – its control by elected officials, the role of a free press, and other institutionalized checks and balances. That is why vigilance is in order when the category is distorted, as it was by the definition used by the African Development Bank in 2011. As we have already seen, two-thirds of the ADB's 'middle class', those who earn only between 2 and 5 dollars a day, hardly have time to engage in day-to-day politics.

In Nigeria, which is the best showcase for contemporary sub-Saharan Africa, the first American-style shopping mall was inaugurated in Lagos in 2005. Since then, for the 20 million inhabitants of this megacity, only a handful of large commercial centres have opened their doors. That says something significant about the purchasing power of the local consumer market. Nevertheless, using an income measure of 15 or more dollars per day per family, the Nigerian middle class is expected to triple over the next two decades, growing from around 25 million consumers today to some 75 million in 2030. Continent-wide, the World Bank predicts a quadrupling of the middle class within the same time horizon. Other upheavals of similar magnitude to the mobile telephone revolution are also likely to occur. In 2014, Africans spent 10 per cent of their income on their cellular phones. In Western Europe, if the proportion of per capita income were the same, that would be the equivalent of a telephone bill of more than 350 euros per month *on average*. Given the proximity of most Africans to subsistence level, spending that much money to communicate is hard to understand, aside from falling back on the threadbare cliché of 'Africa, the continent of oral tradition'. Yet there are plenty of rational explanations: the telephone can take the place of travel in countries where travel is both costly and gruelling; it allows the vast majority of the population who do not own a computer to access the internet; and it permits the digital natives on the continent – Africa's abundant youth cohort – to upend the age hierarchy thanks to their understanding of new opportunities such as e-banking. In Kenya, the most advanced African country in terms of electronic transactions, the equivalent of half the country's GNP is transacted via mobile phones. Two-thirds of the population use some 37,000 digital 'kiosks' to store or transfer their money, known as *pesa* in Swahili, which provides the name for one of the biggest commercial services offered by Safaricom, M-Pesa. This constitutes an everyday revolution, representing huge progress for large numbers of people. Still, the absence of a classic banking system is a significant drawback. In Kenya, 80 per cent of the population do not have a bank account, which makes it difficult if not impossible for the country's size-able middle class to acquire real estate. In 2013, out of 44 million inhabitants, only 22,000 people obtained a mortgage (Olopade 2014: 143).

Identity as a Repertoire

In his novella-length story, 'Luxurious Hearses',[5] the Nigerian writer Uwem Akpan recounts the escape of a young boy from a town in northern Nigeria after an outbreak of religious riots. The son of a Christian father from the southeast and a Muslim mother from the north – his parents are separated – Gabriel aka Jubril is caught in the crossfire. He gets on one of the last buses out of town, filled with Christians trying to return south to their homeland. But though Gabriel/Jubril has purchased a ticket with Luxurious Buses, his seat is occupied by an old, traditional chief who refuses to give it up. Two young women intervene and remonstrate with the man; a third, older and more dignified, tries to reason with the chief, whose age and rank have given him an exaggerated sense of self-importance. But he refuses to budge. Both embittered and nostalgic for the bygone era of military regimes, which typically paid off traditional chiefs with oil revenue in return for controlling their subjects, he launches into a tirade against democracy, the great leveller of the distinctions on which he relies for pre-eminence. Bedlam ensues, and the bus is transformed into a rolling, raucous debating society with sound arguments and, more often than not, fallacious points made in bad faith. Gabriel/Jubril is doubly handicapped. First, he dares not speak for fear his accent will reveal that he grew up in the north. Secondly, his right hand has been amputated at the wrist after he was caught stealing. He must keep it concealed to avoid being identified by his Christian fellow passengers as a Muslim who has been punished according to *sharia* law. In addition, Jubril is uncomfortable in the presence of unveiled women, whom – as a result of his Muslim upbringing – he views as shameless and indecent. Slowly, however, the Gabriel in him gains the upper hand and gets accustomed to their presence. But the TV screen on the bus, positioned just over his head – a source of flickering light by which the violent acts he is fleeing continue to pursue him, stoking the anti-Islamic sentiments of his fellow passengers to a fever pitch – is an inexhaustible source of torment.

The symbolism of these cramped, closed quarters is obvious: like Nigeria, the bus has fewer seats than passengers. And it is not enough to have your ticket, the equivalent of a vote at the ballot box, to take your rightful place. You have to fight for it, win over rivals, form alliances with third parties, all the while running the gamut of identity politics. This process pits men against women, young people against old people, the poor against the rich, civilians against the military, the governing elite against the governed masses, democratic stalwarts against military apologists,

southerners against northerners, Christians against Muslims . . .
Gabriel/Jubril panics at the casualness with which everyone else
on the bus is switching sides. If 'Hell is other people', as Sartre
contended in his play *No Exit*, Gabriel/Jubril fails to understand
that otherness is not a massive block of irreconcilable difference
but a contested repertoire of individual or collective markers.
Command of this repertoire separates winners from losers, and
even the living from the dead in times of collective madness like
these. In the end, Gabriel/Jubril gives himself away, and is killed
without mercy. His body is dumped by the roadside while the
cargo hold of the bus is filled with 'good' Christian dead, destined for the eternal resting grounds of their ancestors. This is
the origin of the title of the story, a derisive critique of a country
more worried about the dead and the afterlife than the living and
the present.

Through the various exchanges that take place on the bus,
and the shifting geometry of alliances that result, readers are led
to amend their initial viewpoint: it is not difference per se that
causes conflict, but conflicting *interests* disguised as differences –
the political weaponization of otherness – that generate enmity.
Clashing interests invest in empty shells called 'identities', which
they inhabit under false pretences to cover their nakedness. The
longer a conflict lasts, the more its outward manifestations are
confused with its actual reality. The piling up of victims in the
violent struggles between Christians and Muslims hollows out an
even larger gulf between the two communities, giving credence to
the idea that 'they are not made to get along'. By the same token,
in countries like Rwanda and Burundi where the principal cleavage is ethnicity, the long history of massacres between Hutus and
Tutsis fosters the belief that the two groups do not know how
to live together in peace. This belief ultimately becomes its own
reality. The deaths of the past weigh on the present, and this pressure incites each side to kill pre-emptively for fear of being killed.
But Hutus and Tutsis are no more condemned to murder each
other in perpetuity than, say, Catholics and Protestants are in

Ireland or the supporters of the House of Plantagenet and those of the House of Valois were during the Hundred Years' War in the fourteenth and fifteenth centuries – even though for a long time that seemed to be the case.

For a long time, too, it was assumed that ethnicity was the 'natural' and most important cleavage in Africa, an atavistic impulse driving the continent's turmoil. But in the geopolitical context that took shape after 11 September 2001, and the 'global war against terrorism', religion has returned as a vector of conflict mobilization. At the same time, (post-)electoral violence has multiplied, a sign of the increasing importance of the ballot box. Clashes over access to water or control of arable land or pasture have also become more frequent. But isn't conflict in Africa above all generational, since the continent's exceptional demographic profile has given rise to an unbridgeable divide between a vast number of young people, who have no political voice, and a small minority of elders, who refuse to cede power? One would expect this to be the case. But why then, in 'Luxurious Hearses', is the quarrel over age and its privileges only background noise to the far louder clamour of ethnic and religious conflict? And if inter-generational conflict is not the matrix of confrontation in Africa, in what forms is the wish of the continent's youth to become full persons and assume the mantle of adulthood playing itself out?

Musa Wo, the Legendary 'Enfant Terrible'

Martha Carey, an American anthropologist, worked for the French NGO Médecins sans frontières during the civil war in Sierra Leone from 1993 to 2002. An 'expert beyond experience' in extreme violence, trained to resist 'the anguish of the marrow' and 'see the skull beneath the skin',[6] she sought to understand the atrocities committed by the rebels of the Revolutionary United Front (RUF), who punished civilians with a 'short sleeve' – an arm chopped off at the elbow – or a 'long sleeve' – an amputation at the wrist – to prevent them from 'taking their destiny into their own hands', the slogan used by those who advocated a return to democracy and an end to military rule. In an article entitled 'Survival is Political: History, Violence, and the Contemporary Power Struggle in Sierra Leone', Carey finds a crucial answer in the men's secret society known as *Poro* and its initiation rites. She also reflects on a figure legendary throughout West Africa: Sundiata Keita, a warrior king and founder of the Malian empire in the thirteenth century. According to 'The Epic of Sundiata', of which several versions circulate across the region, the emperor was born a cripple, mocked by everyone for his inability to stand upright or walk. On the eve of his circumcision, however, he wrapped his arms around the branches of a baobab tree and, with superhuman strength, pulled the giant tree up by its roots. His feat frightened his half-brother the local king, who chased Sundiata and his mother from the court. Sundiata lived in exile until the day he was called home by his people to help repel an enemy invasion. He defeated the marauders, assumed the throne and acquired a vast empire through conquest.

In Sierra Leone, Sundiata Keita is known by the name of Musa Wo. His legend – peppered with cruelties, swindles and frauds – glorifies chaos. He is an 'enfant terrible', a monster both obscene and immoral, yet irresistible. He is the vigorous, ebullient incarnation of youth eluding the control of their elders in a carnivalesque world that has been turned upside down. 'In the evolution of the war and the composition of the ranks of the various armed movements, the stimuli of class, ethnicity and economic category take a back seat to the older, deeper divisions between senior and junior generations', writes Carey (2006: 107). She is talking specifically about Sierra Leone but, as we have seen, the small West African country is not alone in featuring a high percentage of young people: the same is true across the continent. If we extrapolate from Carey's analysis, the intergenerational divide would be the mother of all conflicts in Africa.

'Even my father, I will give him a bullet', if – as the phrase implies – our cause requires it (Leonardi 2007: 391). For more than twenty years, some 250,000 young recruits have repeated this chilling phrase as an oath of allegiance in training camps run by the Sudan People's Liberation Army (SPLA). Between the beginning of the second civil war in Sudan, in 1983, and the peace agreement between the North and the South in 2005, these young soldiers vowed to go as far as parricide to bring about liberation. Could there be a starker expression of intergenerational conflict? Yet Cherry Leonardi, an Africanist at the University of Durham, has challenged this explanation. In a 2007 paper, she warned that 'the danger of explaining all youth mobilization for violence in terms of an African youth crisis is not only that it ignores the specific local reasons for resentment and rebellion, but also that it detaches youth from their families and communities by treating them as a distinct marginalized entity' (2007: 411).

After a two-year investigation in the field, Leonardi reached the conclusion that the goal of young South Sudanese was not to leave their home and join the ranks of the SPLA in a bid to overturn generational control. Rather, they sought to navigate the polarized field between their emotional place of origin – their 'home' – and the 'sphere of government' – *hakuma* in Arabic – that includes the world of political rivalries. The SPLA as well as the central government in Khartoum are all part of *hakuma*, as is the big city whose modernity makes it the antithesis of 'home'. In the final analysis, young South Sudanese had more confidence in their home because it seemed to them ultimately safer than the political sphere, which they found inherently unstable and sometimes downright treacherous. Their main objective was to avoid being exploited, either as minors in their homes or as recruits of the rebel movement. Their goal, says Leonardi, was 'to avoid capture rather than to overcome exclusion', while playing the *hakuma* off against the home, and vice versa: to win in both spheres without confusing the two. 'Youth are often more concerned with retaining their independence than with overcoming marginalization, a reflection of their inherently in-between position' (2007: 406), Leonardi concludes. This 'youthful' strategy resembles a revised version of the myth of Icarus, albeit with a happy ending. To escape the labyrinth where he and his father, Daedalus, are imprisoned, Icarus uses the pair of wings his ingenious father has constructed from wax and feathers. But, despite Daedalus' warning, his hubristic ascent brings him too close to the sun. The South Sudanese sons take off on their own, alone, but heed the fatherly advice . . .

Who between Martha Carey and Cherry Leonardi is right? Does the polarization of generations in Africa – a rift of continental proportions – lead to violent confrontations or carefully managed scenarios of avoidance? On board Luxurious Hearses, the tension between old and young, like those between men and women or the military and civilians, are not fatal, or at least not as immediately fatal as the religious divide, which often leads to death. Is that because these other antagonisms are not particularly relevant? In what situation does one identify first and foremost as 'young', rather than as a woman or a man, a civilian or a soldier, Hausa or Igbo, Muslim or Christian? It is not obvious. In Africa, to be young is the most widely shared condition, and the highest common factor in the sum of identities based on gender, tribe, religion, etc. Therefore, what the American writer George Packer said of Togo in 1984 is true – more than ever – for the entire youth continent: Africa is *The Village of Waiting*.[7] A multitude of young people find themselves abandoned in this continental waiting room of life, but a collective rush towards the door is not necessarily the solution. Their peers are more likely their competitors, and only potentially their allies. Unlike their elders, they have only the ennui of the waiting room to share amongst them. In Zimbabwe, the geriatric former president Robert Mugabe was able to mobilize young people equally as well as, if not better than, the opposition because he had something to offer them, even if it was something in the short term – enrolment in the National Youth Service as a 'green bomber', licence to invade a white-owned farm or to loot international food aid. But the short term is the best you can hope for south of the Sahara, where, more than anywhere else, the long term does not belong to the living.

For a young African, to be independent consists as much in decreasing the influence of fathers *and* peers as increasing one's own margins of possibility by building alliances across the board, and not only within one's own generation. In contemporary Africa, where the principle of seniority has been undermined by an unprecedented population surge, the tension between old and young is the mother not of all conflict, but of *instability*. It is this tension that actualizes itself across the 'politics of resentment', to use a term coined by the American anthropologist Mike McGovern. In his work on Guinea and the Ivory Coast, McGovern describes a modus operandi of youth in terms of a triptych: negation-supplication-play (2011: 67–101, 124–7). In the words of Goethe's Faust, youth is 'the spirit that negates / And rightly so / For all that comes to be / Deserves to perish wretchedly'. At the same time, the young beg the elders to share their privileges with them and to raise them up to a seat at the table. If they don't get what they ask for, the young up-end the table, like Musa Wo, the legendary 'enfant terrible'. However, when their antics degenerate and cause death and destruction or result in punishment, the young deny responsibility and revert to the child-like status they so desperately wish to transcend. 'Only kidding!'

We are now set for a long series of departures. They begin in the African village, which the young leave for the nearest town, before they leave that town for the capital city, and their country's capital for a regional hub and, finally, the regional metropolis for an even brighter place beckoning from further afield, most often Europe. In fact, these stages in the journey constitute a single continuous movement, as Africa's youth strike out in search of a modernity they find hard to lay claim to at home. As the French-Caribbean poet Aimé Césaire put it, 'black youth is turning its back on the tribe of their elders'. He wrote those words in 1935, when Africa – demographically speaking – was just beginning to emerge. 'What does black youth desire?' Césaire asks. 'To live. But to truly live, one must remain oneself.' That is a tall order for people who see it as their destiny to uproot and reinvent themselves elsewhere.

4

A Cascade of Departures

The United Nations monitors four types of global migratory flows: migration between high-income countries, migration between low-income countries, migration from low-income to high-income countries, and migration from high-income to low-income countries. The total number of migrants in the world – that is, the number of persons living in a country that is not their country of birth – has increased from 92 million in 1960 to 258 million in 2017. Although this number has jumped 41 per cent since 2000, when there were 165 million migrants in the world, it still represents only a sliver of the world's population: 3 per cent in 1960 versus 3.4 per cent in 2017. Over that period, however, the world population has more than doubled and the dominant migratory pattern has shifted: while movements within the developing world used to be by far the most important, the flow from the less developed 'Global South' to the more developed 'Global North' has become predominant. In 1960, about 20 million migrants from the South were living in the North, versus 60 million migrants from the South who had made a fresh start in another developing country. But by the end of the century the stock of these South-South migrants had only modestly increased to 80 million, while the stock of South-North migrants had reached 60 million by 2000, and 140 million by 2015. 'High-income countries have absorbed most of the recent growth in the global population of international migrants, gaining sixty-four million of the eighty-five million migrants added worldwide between 2000 and 2017', the UN's International Migration Report indicates (United Nations 2017: 4). According to the International Organization for Migration, 35 per cent of migratory flows in 2015 were South-North movements; 37 per cent were South-South; 5.6 per cent were movements from the developed North to the developing South; while North-North migration stood at 22.6 per cent (IOM 2018). 'So much for the inevitability of globalization leading to an increase in migration: within the rich world, it didn't', says Paul Collier (2013: 50). Taking a historical perspective, one could argue that globalization *avant la lettre* also led to mass migration from what is today the rich North, namely Europe, between 1850 and 1914. But the broader point here is that inhabitants of high-income countries travel frequently abroad but do not settle easily in other countries, even high-income countries. By comparison, inhabitants of low-income countries cross international borders less often to go to and fro, and more often to start a new life elsewhere, increasingly in the North. Put differently: the 'globalizers' tend to travel while the 'globalized' tend to migrate. The globalizers are driving the worldwide process of integration which, in turn, is driving those among the globalized who want to be part of it away from their homes and towards the North. Their desire to move from the periphery to the centre is, at its core, a quest for agency in the modern world.

Between 2000 and 2015, an average of 4.1 million migrants per year moved from the South to a country in the OECD, the world's most developed economic bloc. The United Nations, which provides this data, expects that between 2015 and 2050 some 91 million people from the world's developing nations will move to the world's wealthiest countries, which over the same period should register a net population decline, with 20 million more deaths than births. As a result, it is expected that 82 per cent of their demographic growth will come from immigration. Collier is convinced that, 'for the foreseeable future, international migration will not reach equilibrium: we have been observing the beginnings of disequilibrium of epic proportions' (2013: 50). One might hope that this migratory imbalance will eventually redress another, deeply entrenched disequilibrium, namely global inequity: in 2006, researchers from the United Nations University released data showing that, while the world's richest 10 per cent of adults owned 85 per cent of the world's global household wealth, the bottom half collectively owned barely 1 per cent.[1] Ten years later, the situation had not improved. More than 70 per cent of the world's adults still owned under 100,000 US dollars in assets and held only 3 per cent of global wealth while those owning over 100,000 US dollars totalled only 8.6 per cent of the planet's population but owned 85.6 per cent of global wealth.[2] Given the enormity and the persistence of this gap, how many more times can we tell the marginalized multitudes of the South that they must stay put and wait for development to come their way, as Northern satellite TV beams a flood of images attesting to its opulence into the South? It is a mockery of the poor that takes place around the clock.

This is a familiar argument, and it flows well. But we have to be careful not to be taken in by false evidence. Certainly, the ubiquity of satellite television and increasing internet access sharpen the contrast on the world's poorest continent between lived experience and what is 'seen on the screen' – vicarious experience available through media. But, so far, Africans have not yet stormed the world's citadels of opulence, beginning with Europe, and not only, nor even principally, because they have been reinforced against unauthorized incomers. As the 2015 record migration towards Europe – mainly from Syria, Iraq and Afghanistan – has made clear, the Old Continent is anything but inaccessible, despite its high fences, coils of concertina wire, radar surveillance, naval patrols and digital databases. Sub-Saharan migrants, however, have not yet arrived in truly large numbers at Europe's borders, because the necessary conditions for Africa's 'scramble for Europe' have not yet come together. More on this in a moment.

Let us first question the received wisdom that the gap between the North and the South is still growing and driving global inequality. In reality, the divide between rich and poor countries – though still huge – is narrowing. One only needs to compare, for example, the high percentage of unemployed young Italians to the growing cohort of *nouveaux riches* young Brazilians, or the number of upwardly mobile Chinese entrepreneurs to the number of Greek business owners in sudden free fall. Even south of the Sahara, where the world map of 'rich Northerners' and 'poor Southerners' might seem a reliable geographical projection of global inequality, the rise of a local middle class and the ongoing, unbridled enrichment of the postcolonial elite tend to exacerbate *national* disparities. In his 2012 book *The Globalization of Inequality*, François Bourguignon, the former chief economist of the World Bank and later head of the Paris School of Economics, made this point convincingly. He showed that the per capita income gap between the North and the South, which had been steadily growing since the beginning of the nineteenth century, peaked in 1980 – not coincidentally the moment when a new and powerful impetus for worldwide integration was given the name 'globalization'. Since then, the North-South income gap has reversed itself to the point of coming close to where it was in 1900. At the same time, *national* income disparities have grown vastly in both the North and the South. However, the context of this new wealth polarization is different in each bloc. In large parts of Latin America and Asia, hundreds of millions of people have lifted themselves out of absolute poverty, while in tradition-ally wealthy countries of the North, the least qualified workers – increasingly exposed to international competition – have sunk into the 'precariat', the modern-day global proletariat, less and less insulated from economic unpredictability.

In the words of the German philosopher Peter Sloterdijk, they have lost their 'civilizational rent' – the kind of annuity they had previously received due only to the fact of having been born in the 'right' place. In an interview published on 11 May 2017 in the French weekly *Le Point*, Sloterdijk explained:

> Populism, whether on the Left or the Right, . . . translates the resentment stemming from the loss of a number of privileges that had been granted even to the low-income classes in Europe since the 1950s. They benefited from a sort of 'civilizational rent': it sufficed to be born, for example, in France or Germany, to enjoy a considerable advantage over competitors in India or China. In those days, even unqualified European workers could afford a house, a car, a middle-class lifestyle. At that particular moment of economic history – a precarious, untenable moment – they were awarded a premium payment for the simple fact of being French or German. . . . But as globalization went on, this European premium has been dissolved.

So has America's imperial rent, as the election of Donald Trump attests. Today, the West shares with 'the rest' the fact that wealth no longer divides the world into rich and poor nations as much as it separates the winners and losers of globalization *in each country*. Africa, unfortunately, is the only part of the world that has so far lost out on both counts: its internal disparities have dramatically increased, while at the same time it has not gained enough ground relative to the standard of living in the developed world due to its population growth and the law of large numbers.

Regarding South-North migratory flows, another analytical assumption needs to be challenged. It views migration through a postcolonial lens alone and overestimates the 'magnetism' that attracts the inhabitants of former colonies to the old metropoles. Using a biological metaphor, some – mostly francophone

– analysts speak of a 'postcolonial tropism'. No doubt they have a point: familiarity with the language and culture of their former colonizer makes settling in the UK, France, Belgium or Portugal significantly easier for many Africans, depending on where they were born. But this familiarity is dwindling as generations succeed one another with astonishing speed in a part of the world where, under current conditions, half of the population is 'renewed' every eighteen years. What is more, Africa's youthful demographic profile, in combination with globalization, favours the 'Americanization' of the continent, even in its non-English-speaking parts. America's soft power – in particular its youth culture and Black America's protest culture – is in tune with African modernity, its pioneering spirit, the existential bricolage and massive recourse to self-help in societies where new codes of conduct have to be reimagined from the ground up by the young, with few older mentors to assist them.

Abidjan's most coveted suburb is called Beverly Hills, not Neuilly, and fast food and 'gangsta rap' reign supreme among the young, which, south of the Sahara, is to say almost everyone. At the same time, in former French colonies, strong anti-French sentiments have come to prevail, probably in response to the long tutelary shadow that Paris cast over them well beyond their formal independence across three decades of the Cold War and, as some would argue, up until the present day. Far from representing a welcome familiarity, this 'shared history' is precisely the reason some francophone migrants, above all intellectuals and disaffected members of the elite, wouldn't want to live anywhere near France. More broadly, the new generation of well-informed Africans sees the world for what it is today. They know that it is Germany – rather than Great Britain or France – that carries the real weight in Europe, and America and China in the world.

In addition, a wholesale negativity – miserabilism – about Africa, this 'hell' that 'the poor' seek to escape from to reach the European 'paradise', is as treacherous as a trompe l'oeil. Not only does this biased perception ignore the Beverly Hills of Africa, it also fails to explain why there wasn't massive African immigration during the Cold War, when the continent was poorer than it is today and suffered from pervasive tyranny – the bloody rule of dictators like Idi Amin Dada, Mobutu Sese Seko, Francisco Macías Nguema or the self-proclaimed Central African 'Emperor' Jean-Bedel Bokassa. If poverty and oppression were the mainspring of migration, the recurrent droughts and famines in the Sahel region and the Horn of Africa, or the quasi-permanent crisis in the former Belgian Congo (DRC today), would have emptied out a good part of the continent a long time ago. At the very least, this should have happened by the 1990s, when thirty-five African countries were in the midst of some war or another, and millions of civilians were killed (Brunel 2014: loc. 969). Yet the repercussions of Africa's post-Cold War decade for Europe went largely unnoticed. They seemed more or less in line with the steady rise of migratory flows from Africa since the 1960s.

Not everyone in Africa who wishes to migrate to Europe can simply pack up and head out – that much is clear. But what does it actually take to up sticks and leave? Crucially, a deep frustration with the place one is in, and profound disbelief in the prospect of things taking a turn for the better within one's own lifetime. Whether or not the West's blanket assumptions about Africa are exaggerated, large-scale migrations tend to originate from places where there is no hope. And while Western media closely monitor the economic ups and downs of the poorest continent, most Africans know that a slight improvement or decline here or there will not make much of a difference. They see fifty-four shades of grey in a colourful world. And that is precisely the second prerequisite for a definitive departure: being able to look beyond Africa. One has to have a broad horizon to imagine a new life in a far-away place. Africans who have seldom left their village, or for whom visiting a relative in a big city is a great adventure, are unlikely to dream of laying down new roots in London, Rome or Paris. Poverty is more than material deprivation. It imposes tunnel vision on people who must expend their energy to provide for themselves and their children day-in day-out. 'Bare life', to use the term coined by the Italian philosopher Giorgio Agamben, doesn't allow for adventure. Finally, migration comes at a cost. Having the financial means to undertake the long trip to Europe is the sine qua non for leaving Africa. Depending on where one is departing from and headed to, and the challenges of the often-clandestine voyage, the initial sum ranges between 2,000 and 3,000 US dollars – the yearly per capita income in many sub-Saharan countries. So, rather than the 'poorest of the poor', it is a less indigent stratum of Africans – the continent's emerging middle class – that migrates.

The Dilemma of Development Aid

If we set aside the ecological stress that is sure to increase migratory pressures, there are two major conditions that must be met to trigger the 'scramble for Europe' that this book foresees. The first is that a critical mass of Africans must cross the threshold of minimum prosperity, even while a very large income gap between Africa and Europe persists. This will exercise its own attraction on a multitude of young Africans who are able to put aside the tidy sum that is needed to leave, or raise the funds – often with the help of their extended family – that constitute the seed money for their enterprise. For these young Africans, migration is a rite of passage akin to the quest for the Golden Fleece of Jason and the Argonauts. In Greek mythology, Jason and fifty other young men leave on board the Argo to beat back a challenge by the usurper Pelias, who has toppled Jason's father, the legitimate king. In an attempt to rid himself of the rightful heir to the throne, Pelias promises Jason that he will step down if Jason returns with the ultimate prize, the fleece, from Colchis, a fabulously wealthy land situated on the uncertain periphery of the known world. Against all expectations, Jason succeeds. His voyage is a long detour made in order for him to assert his right to govern his country. For young Africans, migration is a similarly epic quest. But while they send home the better part of the riches they find, they themselves only rarely return to a position of power in their native countries.

The second major condition for a quantum leap in the number of Africans leaving for Europe is the existence of African diasporas on the Old Continent. 'Outpost communities of larger population reservoirs elsewhere', as the anthropologist Fredrik Barth defined diasporas (1969: 21), act as bridges. For African migrants, they connect the two sides of the Mediterranean. The presence of 'relatives' in the broadest sense greatly reduces the uncertainty and cost of settling in a European country. Diasporic communities provide a ready-made source of hospitality, support, orientation, connections and sometimes even a first job. They are a sort of airlock allowing migrants to pass from their initial state of confusion to a basic level of familiarity with their new home. Since the 1980s, the presence of a small group of Somali businessmen in the Twin Cities of Minneapolis-Saint Paul in Minnesota has led, some thirty years later, to the biggest concentration of Somalis in the United States – more than 25,000 out of a total of 85,000 in the entire country. In northwestern Germany, Eschweiler, a small town with 55,000 inhabitants, has become a rallying point for several hundred Togolese, out of a total of 14,000 immigrants to Germany from the *Musterkolonie* – 'model colony' – in West Africa, which Berlin ruled from 1884 to 1914. In former metropoles such as Great Britain, France or Belgium, African diasporas are plentiful but often perceived exclusively as a postcolonial phenomenon. In *The Return of the Caravels*, the Portuguese novelist António Lobo Antunes imagined the reversal of colonial history half a millennium after the lateen-rigged ships first allowed the Portuguese to sail against Africa's trade winds and settle on the Angolan and Mozambican coasts. Even though African migrants may still feel some combination of acrimony and admiration for their former colonizers, migration is not simply the unintended consequence of colonialism. In today's globalized world, African migrants go everywhere and on any makeshift boat.

Here is the first paradox: the harder it is for a diaspora to merge into its host country, the more effective that diaspora is in welcoming new immigrants who, in turn, will be more difficult to integrate as they find a 'home away from home' (Collier 2013: 91). The neighbourhood nicknamed Little Somalia in Minneapolis-Saint Paul, the Chinatowns of many large American cities, Peckham in London, Matongé in Brussels and Montreuil on the outskirts of Paris make it much easier for other Somalis, Chinese, Nigerians, Congolese and Malians to 'make landfall'. After that, it is a question of one's point of view: some will be happy that a built-in community assistance network helps newcomers in many different ways; others will deplore these 'foreign enclaves' that merely complicate everyone else's lives. The fact is that a diaspora that persists in maintaining its boundaries, whether by choice or necessity, encourages other migrants from its community of origin to come to a country where they benefit from its cocooning effects but are less likely to become fully integrated citizens.

The term 'diaspora' refers to an expression of unease that persists in a new place, where people refuse to accept the present in the name of the past. Literally, it refers to a 'dispersion', such as the one brought about by the slave trades or the deportation of the Jews to Babylon following the destruction of the Temple of Jerusalem at the end of the sixth century BC. To call yourself a member of a diaspora is to lay claim to the status of a castaway of history, a victim: you have ended up somewhere as a result of misfortune, if not worse – in any event against your will. This was the lot, for example, of Armenian survivors of the genocide of 1915–16 in Turkey, and is the lot today in Africa of exiled Rwandan dissidents who would fear for their lives if they stayed in their country. But it is not the case for the vast majority of African migrants. They do not flee imminent danger to their life. They try to escape circumstances that, certainly, are often difficult. But others around them decide, on the contrary, to stay, and it would be a mistake to confer victim status, en masse, on those who flee life in Africa rather than stay and face its challenges. Similarly, it is misguided in my view to ascribe a collective form of 'ontological exceptionalism' to African migrants – or for them to claim victimization as their permanent condition. Why, for example, should Malian immigrants in France, even those who have become naturalized French citizens, always remain part of a diaspora – be it Malian, African or simply 'black' – while, say, Italian or Portuguese immigrants do not? And why should their children, who hold French citizenship by birthright? Only African migrants are locked up in their past, a perpetual 'return to pain' – the literal meaning of the word 'nostalgia' – which prevents them from living their lives fully in the here and now. This danger has become even greater since the advent of free and universal technologies of communication. In the past, the bridges between the migrant's former and newfound country were mostly severed. The physical exigencies of life required the newcomer to look ahead into the future in his new home. Now, the immigrant resembles Janus, the Roman god with two faces, also the god of entryways and ports. He looks both forward and back, standing watch over beginnings and uncertain ends and difficult passages in between.

Here is the second paradox: the countries of the North subsidize the countries of the South with development aid so that the poor can live better lives and – though this is rarely said so directly – stay where they are. By doing so, however, rich countries shoot themselves in the foot. In effect, at least initially, they provide a bonus for potential migrants by helping poor countries attain the threshold of prosperity, at which point their citizens have the means to leave and live elsewhere. This is the dilemma of co-development, which claims to be a 'win-win' for North and South but in reality provides the poor in the South with the means to join the rich in the North.[3] There is no perfect solution. In the long term, a prosperous Africa is not only desirable per se but also the best rationale for Africans to stay in their countries. Until then, however, development aid subsidizes migration. Only cynics will find comfort in the fact that aid is rarely effective, especially in Africa.

In his reportage entitled 'The Uninvited', published in 2000 in *The London Review of Books*, Jeremy Harding, a contributing editor at the LRB, noted with some irony the dilemma of development aid:

> Wealthy states – EU member states, for instance – who hope to discourage migration from very poor parts of the world by a cautious transfer of resources (more advantageous bilateral trade deals, deeper debt relief and so on) should not be downcast if they discover, after a few years, that these initiatives have failed to improve conditions in their target countries. For a country that did indeed show an increase in GDP, adult literacy and life expectancy – a general improvement all round – would be likely to produce even more aspiring migrants than a country trying to cope with live burial at the bottom of the world economy.

Twelve years later, in his book *Border Vigils: Keeping Migrants Out of the Rich World*, Harding drove his point home even more forcefully: 'War, hunger and social breakdown may not have caused massive numbers of people to migrate north beyond the natural boundary of the Sahara, but the first glimmerings of prosperity may well inspire higher numbers of Africans to come to Europe' (2012: loc. 2459–61).

Why? The poorest of the poor cannot afford to migrate. They are too busy making ends meet. At the other extreme, which often coincides with the other end of the world, the well-heeled travel frequently, to the point of believing that neither distance nor borders are of any consequence. Their freedom of movement – a global-minority privilege – blunts their desire to settle elsewhere. That is not the case for those who have narrowly escaped 'bare life', and wish to live in these lands of seemingly unconfined opportunity. 'Rising Africa', a demographic billionaire, is rapidly scaling up its migratory potential: yesterday it lacked the wherewithal to leave; today its population is approaching the threshold of a prosperity that will set it on the road to the European 'paradise'.

The Draining of Lake Chad

Ecological stress – the factor we bracketed out earlier – could shift the current migratory flows out of Africa into an exodus in certain parts of the continent, and crucially in the Sahel region, that vast swath of arid land stretching along the southern edge of the Sahara from Mauritania to Eritrea, which includes parts of Senegal, Mali, Burkina Faso, Niger, Chad and Sudan. In 2015, around 135 million people lived in this zone of some 7 million square kilometres, about a quarter of the entire African continent, the equivalent of three-quarters of the land mass of the United States and thirty-three times the size of Great Britain. The population in the Sahel is on target to hit 330 million by 2050 – seven times its population in 2000, a growth rate which, if applied to the UK, would have seen that country's population soar from 59 million to 413 million. The demographic growth rate in the Sahel region ranges between 2.5 and 3.9 per cent, the fertility rate between 4.1 and 7.6 children per woman – the world's top tier. The per capita GDP, however, is among the lowest, between 700 dollars per year in Eritrea and Niger and 2,000 in Senegal, Mauritania and Sudan.

The demographic pressure that comes to bear upon the Sahel's 'useful' territory – the small portion of land that receives sufficient rain or can be irrigated – is merely one of several interlocking factors in the region that put it under severe ecological stress, along with climate change, desertification, deforestation, erosion, soil depletion and the increasing scarcity of water. The UN's Food and Agriculture Organization (FAO) estimates that 80 per cent of the Sahel's land has been 'degraded' and one-third of its population suffers from chronic malnutrition. Experts differ in their interpretations of the region's erratic rainfall patterns, but there is a scientific consensus that the average temperature will rise by between 3 and 5 degrees Celsius by 2050. That in turn will threaten the subsistence agriculture on which a majority of the population depends. By the middle of the twenty-first century, while the population is set to double, agricultural production in Burkina Faso is expected to drop by 13 per cent and by as much as 50 per cent in Niger, Chad and Sudan. At the same time, an ultra-rapid urbanization – this in the context of a continent that is already urbanizing at a historic pace – is set to occur, heightening the risk of epidemics such as cholera and dengue fever, linked to large concentrations of people living in impoverished circumstances.

'It is hard to believe that this absurd population growth, in a region already confronted by so many handicaps and threats, will not lead to a range of tragedies', writes the French researcher Serge Michaïlof, who is especially interested in the four francophone countries of the Sahel: Burkina Faso, Mali, Niger and Chad (2015: 218).[4] Together, the population of these countries is expected to triple by 2050. They are already living on international charity, which accounts for more than 10 per cent of their GDP, nearly 40 per cent of their tax revenue and between 60 and 90 per cent of their investment budgets. Part of the problem is a fundamental lack of institutional capacity, a constraint that limits the amount of foreign aid the state can absorb. In 2014, according to a report by the International Crisis Group, 'Niger spent little more than half the development aid it received' (2015: 7), despite the country's bottomless poverty and infinite, often urgent needs. Take public education: in a country where 60 per cent of the population is under eighteen years old, 80 per cent of the teachers have had no formal training, secondary school attendance hovers around 30 per cent and post-secondary around 5 per cent, while 80 per cent of state schools do not have drinking water and three-quarters have no toilets. In Niger, the national employment agency provided benefits to about 1,500 jobless workers in 2014, yet 243,000 young people – nearly a quarter of a million – entered the job market that year, competing for around 4,000 jobs in the formal sector. In 2035, there will be 572,000 newcomers entering the job market – 'a precise figure because these future workers have already been born', Michaïlof adds (2015: 91). On the whole, the outlook for the francophone heartland of the Sahel region is bleak.

Ecological stress is a double challenge for good governance: in the short term, leaders face the urgent task of limiting its impact; in the long term, they must try to eliminate or mitigate its causes. In this regard, it is often argued that Africa is not a major polluter, accounting only for 4 per cent of human greenhouse gas emissions. But it is 'precisely because Africa today is the largest part of the world suffering from poverty and a lack of industrialization, that it will win hands down any competition for fastest growing energy needs over the next fifty years', according to Jean-Michel Severino and Olivier Ray, the co-authors of *Africa's Moment*. 'So it is also in Africa where the battle against global warming will play out' (Severino and Ray 2010: loc. 3778). And this battle has already started. The proliferation of diesel generators, the burning of garbage, the use of charcoal for cooking, the old and dilapidated vehicles with little or no emissions controls, all combine across Africa in a manner so disastrous that the OECD, in a study published in 2016, admits that 'we simply do not know the consequences over the next few decades'.[5] The demographers Jean-Claude Chasteland and Jean-Claude Chesnais estimate that 'countries in the midst of catching up with the rest of the world will only increase tension on energy markets and hence deepen environmental fears. But the crucial question will remain that of water: today, only 18 per cent of the world's population has access to safe drinking water and to a proper sewage system' (2006: 1015).

Only certain areas in Africa – most notably the Congo Basin – can hope to cash in on a 'green rent' in the future, whereas most other parts of the continent will be the principal victims of climate change. Among the ten nations that are most vulnerable to global warming, seven are African: the Central African Republic, Eritrea, Ethiopia, Nigeria, Sierra Leone, Chad and Sudan. Rising sea levels threaten 250 million people living along the African coasts, especially the West African shoreline where the urban sprawl between the Ghanaian capital Accra and the Nigerian megacity Lagos is about to merge into one giant conurbation stretching 500 kilometres, and likely to have about 50 million inhabitants by 2035. Rural inhabitants in Africa's interior are equally threatened. Two-thirds of Africa's farmers, fishermen and hunters are dependent on the continent's natural resources, and bear the brunt of environmental degradation in all its forms, from lack of firewood through leaky oil pipelines, poaching and toxic waste dumps, to overfishing by large commercial fleets.

Because it is subject to so many variables, the impact of eco-logical stress is difficult to predict. Some estimates anticipate 200 million 'climate refugees' worldwide by 2050. But at this stage, any global figure is a long shot. Only specific adumbrate the shape of things to come. Lake Chad offers a case study with reliable indicators. Environmental degradation in and around the lake already affects some 30 million people in Nigeria, Niger, Chad and Cameroon. In the 1960s, this large and shallow endorheic water mass – a closed hydraulic system that does not flow into a river or the sea – extended across 25,000 square kilometres. Today it covers no more than one tenth of that area and, without a major initiative, could disappear entirely in the next twenty years. 'The Congo River Basin, which is the lungs of humanity, is going to be invaded by Sahelians who will seek refuge there', Chad's president Idriss Déby warned at the United Nations Climate Change Conference in Paris in December 2015. One plan that could avoid the catastrophic scenario of Sahelian climate refugees invading Africa's largest tropical rainforest envisages a 1,350 kilometre-long, navigable canal that would divert water from the Ubangi River, one of the main tributaries of the Congo River, and channel it into the Chari-Logon river system that provides Lake Chad with 95 per cent of its water. But that idea is almost as old as the Lake Chad Basin Commission, created in 1964, whose member states are supposed to oversee water usage in the region. So far, international donors have not come up with the money – some 6.5 billion US dollars – necessary to fund the project. And the riparian countries of the Lake Chad Basin have not done their part either. In Chad, for example, the government has responded to the rising number of clashes between pastoral nomads and sedentary peasants with the same, purely military approach that it has been using in the fight against Boko Haram, the Islamist insurgency that has spread from Nigeria across the region. Since 2009, when Boko Haram launched first its local, then regional jihad, some 20,000 people around Lake Chad have been killed and another 2.4 million displaced. Some 7 million people are suffering from famine in an increasingly precarious ecosystem. Rampant environmental degradation combines with a vicious fight to establish a caliphate. In the four countries – Nigeria, Niger, Chad and Cameroon – territory bordering Lake Chad constitutes the outer periphery of their national administrations. Northeastern Nigeria, for instance, where Boko Haram first emerged, is the least developed of the country's seven official 'zones', no matter the metric used, from per capita GDP to infant mortality to the literacy rate. In this densely populated area without resources, millions of unschooled young people find refuge in *madrasas*, where they memorize Koranic verses and survive as *talibés* or, the Nigerian term, *almajiri*: student beggars of alms.

To Live the 'White Man's Life'

In its attempt to close the gap that separates it from the rest of the world, Africa has engaged in a headlong rush from its villages and cities, national capitals and regional centres to London, Paris, Brussels, Lisbon, New York, the 'Chocolate City' of Guangzhou, and many other places, including small towns in Europe, America and Asia. In sub-Saharan Africa, even more than in the rest of the world, the notion of a 'national' culture is illusory, and so this journey is always in essence the same – a quest for agency, though the ways in which the Golden Fleece is retrieved may differ greatly.[6] In leaving the familiar for the unknown, migrants trade substance for shadow, the real for the unknown. They choose hope over a status quo – with its lack of opportunities, routine and, often, boredom – which they consider worse than the uncertainty of leaving home. Their choice is always more than a simple economic calculus. Charles Piot, my colleague in the Cultural Anthropology department at Duke, offered young men in Kuwdwé, a village in the north of Togo and the site of his fieldwork, the same motorbike that they could have acquired by working extremely hard for several months in a plantation in Nigeria. But Piot's offer was conditional: to earn a bike they had to remain in the village and help their parents in the fields. But they refused. Why? 'Adventure' is the password of migration. Young Africans leave their village, their town or their continent because they hope to catch 'a bit of luck'. As youngsters say in Tambacounda, the largest city in eastern Senegal: *Barsa walla barsac*, Wolof for 'Barcelona or death' (Barcelona, with its dream football team, is shorthand for Europe). Young Africans go for broke, they want to vanquish the world; they accept that they may perish in the process, as long as they do so in Universal Coordinated Time, in sync with the rest of the world.

The first stage of African migration is the rural exodus or, as we might also call it, urban magnetism. Indeed, there is as much 'push' as 'pull' in this mass movement that has been in full flow since the mid-twentieth century. Strikingly, neither the departure nor arrival is ever definitive. Young Africans who are contesting the traditional order in the villages – the hierarchy of age – leave to 'remake' themselves in cities where most of them will find neither adequate housing nor a decent job. Little wonder they don't burn their bridges. Most of them will return regularly. Those who end up finding prosperity and a career in the city will build a new home in the village as a testimony to their success. Far from disavowing their origins, they are revitalized by them. For their part, the crafty old masters of the village prefer to organize what they cannot prevent. They are keenly aware that their authority is better served when those who have left are seen as emissaries – ambassadors from their communities to the wider world – rather than dissident figures or runaway children. And besides, the return home is attended by 'gifts': a village clinic funded by a former 'angry young man' who is now a staid government official or business manager, a school paid for by a successful politician, money remitted back home by one-time villagers now living abroad. In his book about African youth, *The Outcast Majority*, Marc Sommers recalls a visit to a programme for demobilized soldiers in a small village in the Ituri province in northeastern DRC involving about twenty young men and, to his surprise, one middle-aged woman. Intrigued, Sommers approached her during a break and, enquiring in Swahili about her wartime experience, discovered that she wasn't a former combatant but had come on behalf of her son. 'Where is he now?' Sommers asked the woman. '*Mjini*', she replied in Swahili, 'In the city'. 'And why has he gone there?' Sommers continued. '*Maisha ya kizungu*', she explained, 'The white man's life' (Sommers 2015: loc. 1835–40). A more concise account of the driving force behind Africa's migratory movements is hard to imagine, although this doesn't mean that migration is mimicry. Africans do not take to the road striving to imitate Europeans. In this regard, they resemble my German mother who, for her entire life, professed a desire to 'live like God in France', the epitome of happiness for her, though she was neither a believer nor a Francophile.

Africans were leaving their homes long before 'the white man' arrived. It would even appear that in precolonial Africa, something like a 'kinetic lifestyle' was the rule rather than the exception, even among non-nomadic groups. Mobility made borders – in the sense of demarcations that need to be constantly redefined and renegotiated between those on the 'inside' and those on the 'outside' – more fluid than today's actual boundaries. Precolonial migrations clearly provide a historical context

of sorts today. If Malians were over-represented during the first
wave of African immigrants arriving in France in the 1970s,
the most likely explanation can be found in their long migratory experience in West Africa and, in particular, their seasonal
migration from the southeast of Mali to the groundnut basin in
Senegal, where they found work. In the 1970s, a few ventured
further afield and found employment as street sweepers in Paris,
and the rest is a classic example of chain migration. Today, with
one-third of its population living outside the country – the vast
majority somewhere else in West Africa – Mali ranks among
the top countries whose major export is migrant labour. But
the African champion is Cape Verde, an archipelago of volcanic
islands off the coast of Mauritania and Senegal: denied any natural resources, the diaspora of this former Portuguese colony is
estimated at 700,000 people, against an in-country population of
just 600,000.

To move from the village to a big city and, even more so, to
find oneself overnight in the capital, involves a radical change
of scenery, an almost complete recalibration of the migrant's
daily habits and codes of conduct. At the beginning of the rural
exodus, before Africa's wave of independence in the 1960s, new
arrivals – still coming in relatively modest numbers – found a new
home in mixed neighbourhoods adjacent to the European centre,
often named 'the Plateau' because it was built on higher ground
in order to avoid the pools of stagnant water that were a breeding ground for malaria. In Abidjan, for example, the former '*ville
blanche*' was ringed by quarters such as Treichville or Marcory,
where small houses were built around a big, common court-
yard – the seedbed of a new, cosmopolitan lifestyle that emerged
from living side by side, day-in day-out. But as migratory flows
surged, these neighbourhoods could no longer absorb the mass of
newcomers, who started to settle together in satellite towns like
Yopougon, where the Bétés and others from western Ivory Coast
went to live, or Abobo, where the Dyula and others from the
north moved. This chequered history of urbanization goes some

way to explaining the paradox that makes the African city both an incubator of urbanity – a fascinating mélange of linguistic, religious, musical, culinary and sartorial traditions – and a breeding ground for a politicized ethnicity much more visceral than a villager's knee-jerk wariness of the unknown.

'Reasonable number' of newcomers; 'an acceptable pace'; 'absorption capacity'; 'threshold of tolerance' – these are the hollow phrases that litter the discourse of immigration. In absolute terms, as much for the village deprived of its inhabitants as for the city overwhelmed by their arrival, there is a point of equilibrium that amounts to a 'win-win' situation for all concerned: a golden medium allowing the Argonauts to return, perhaps even bearing the Golden Fleece, to a lively village, and the building of bridges within the city for better purposes than simply leapfrogging over slums. But in reality, regulation proves to be impossible each time governments seek to impose it. The 'return to the village' is a chestnut in Africa, an all-too-common refrain, older but just as hackneyed as the Euro-African 'development aid'. Wild dreams are resistant to regulation. In 1983, towards the end of the long reign of Tanzanian president Julius Nyerere, the *Nguvu Kazi* (Hard Work) campaign – to bring unemployed youth back to the villages – ended in total failure. Nowhere – neither in Khartoum nor Lagos nor Harare – has the bulldozing of sprawling slums achieved its goal of convincing their former inhabitants to return to their villages. On the rare occasions when penury and hunger drive them back to the countryside, it is clear that their villages are no longer really 'home'. In Sierra Leone, in particular, city dropouts returning to their rural birthplaces were regarded as 'spoilt brats' even more terrible than the legendary Musa Wo. They filled the ranks of the Revolutionary United Front (RUF) and routinely hacked off the limbs of their compatriots. In January 1999, during an offensive against the capital Freetown, they burned many people alive in their houses in a revenge killing spree known as 'Operation No Living Thing'.

The Repertoire of Rejection

The second stage of African migration, beyond the provincial towns or national capitals, leads to the major regional hubs such as Abidjan, Lagos, Nairobi or Johannesburg. For the first time, an international border is crossed and migrants are faced with a host of new questions involving their official status. Extraneity – the condition of the outsider, and the unfamiliarity and disorientation that are a part of it – is no longer just a lived experience; it is also a legal reality. In a curious misunderstanding of 'Pan-Africanism', Westerners tend to play down the legal implications and 'otherness' involved in intra-African migration as if black people in black Africa were bound to 'naturally' get along; as if certain rights were not the privilege of nationals only and special duties were not incumbent on immigrants. Often those same 'Pan-Africanists' have a tendency to mark as racist any opposition outside of Africa to the arrival of African migrants. Yet the repertoire of negative reactions towards foreigners – or simply more foreigners – is the same south of the Sahara as it is elsewhere, ranging from a reasoned refusal to murder.

A number of contrasting experiences south of the Sahara help to understand that there is a link between the rights and protections accorded to immigrants, on the one hand, and border surveillance and the politics of integration on the other. Border control causes problems pretty much everywhere in sub-Saharan Africa due to many countries' extensive frontiers and the endemic corruption of border agents. In Nigeria, at the end of the oil boom, the overnight expulsion of several hundred thousand foreigners in two large waves – in 1983 and 1985 – was a brutal way of bringing down immigration levels. And since immigrants are easy prey to extortion and administrative abuse, their numbers have henceforth been somewhat self-regulating.

By contrast, during the thirty-three-year reign of Félix Houphouët-Boigny in the Ivory Coast, immigrants from all over West Africa were not only welcomed but given rights nearly equal to those of Ivorian citizens, including the right to vote. To remain viable, this system would have required an efficient border police and a state bureaucracy capable of devising and implementing a clear step-by-step path to citizenship for foreigners – after a given period of residency in the country, or by marriage to an Ivorian, for example. In the absence of such an administrative framework, the Ivorian 'miracle' attracted some 1.3 million immigrants in four years, between 1976 and 1980, to a country that then had only 7 million inhabitants. In 1998, there were 16 million people living in the Ivory Coast, of which 26 per cent were officially classified as 'foreigners'. The term didn't mean much, since this catch-all category did not distinguish among holders of a temporary residence permit or a permanent residence permit, nor between immigrants of the first, second or even third generation. But politically, in the 1990s, when the country was suffering from a prolonged economic crisis and the uncertainties of the post-Houphouët order, the cry of 'one-quarter foreigners' was the equivalent of a fragmentation bomb. We know how it ended: the venomous quarrel about the concept of 'Ivority' – determining who exactly is 'Ivorian' and what this means substantively – led to civil war.

The Ivorian crisis created 'boomerang effects' in several neighbouring countries that had been exporting their labour force to the Ivory Coast, particularly Burkina Faso. Some 1.5 million Burkinabés had been living there. Caught in the crossfire of civil war, several hundred thousand of them returned 'home'. For many, however, including long-term residents as well as those actually born on Ivorian soil, Burkina Faso was no longer truly their home country. Which is exactly what the 'tenga' – 'those who remained on the soil of their birth' – did not hesitate to make clear to the 'kosweogo' – 'those who had lived abroad'. In 2002, Burkina Faso mounted 'Operation Bayiri', or 'the return to the homeland', to come to the rescue of its many nationals eager to flee the fighting in the Ivory Coast. But six years later, at the end of 2008, the Burkinabé authorities had a radical change of heart. After riots broke out in the country's biggest cities to protest against 'the "pretensions", showy attitude and criminality' (Beucher 2009: 100) of its repatriated fellow citizens, the government – via posters and TV spots – tried to reassure the *tenga* that 'to be Burkinabé must be earned'.

In 2000, Jeremy Harding wondered whether 'the power of attraction' that South Africa exercised on the rest of the continent was not the reason 'why, finally, there are so few sub-Saharan hands clinging to the portcullis' of fortress Europe. Since then, the post-apartheid 'rainbow nation' has lost much of its attractiveness. In the early 2000s, the number of deportations sharply increased. By 2005, about 150,000 Zimbabweans alone had been expelled (Hiropoulos 2017: 1). And since 2008 a series of violent and sometimes deadly attacks against African immigrants have occurred in several South African townships. In 2018, after years of debate, South Africa adopted a new immigration law that, among other things, no longer allows holders of long-term residency visas automatic citizenship, and introduces a point system designed to bring in highly qualified migrants. This legislation enshrines what advocates of stricter admission requirements would want in Europe as well, except that even they would never call such a reform 'Clean Sweep'. That the ANC in South Africa believes it is especially necessary to do some 'house cleaning' lends weight to Harding's idea that the rainbow nation has long served as a receptacle for the continent's migratory overflow, especially from neighbouring countries that are members of the Southern African Development Community (SADC). But no one knows by any measure of certainty how many immigrants are today living in South Africa. Unsubstantiated claims of 1.5 million Zimbabweans, and 'almost a third of Malawi's population' (if this were true, it would be a figure close to 6 million people), cohabit with painstakingly compiled data that put the number of foreigners – all categories taken together, including the elusive illegal residents – at between 2 and 3 million, a relatively small fraction of South Africa's total population of 57 million (Hiropoulos 2017: 1).

The last stage of African migration leads from the continent's villages, towns, cities, capitals and regional hubs to points overseas. Crossing the Mediterranean, or an even larger ocean, represents a formidable obstacle for the African migrant. But before turning our attention to the trial of the journey to Europe, let us take stock of the insights provided by intra-African migration. In the first place, there are many false starts, and no arrival is definitive, unless there is a permanent rupture with the migrant's birthplace. Most of the time, between the village and the town, or between the migrant's native country and a different, more prosperous African state, there is a back and forth. On each occasion, the migrant seems to echo the words of the French playwright and musician Jean Tardieu: 'If I left without looking back, I would soon lose sight of myself.' In addition – and this is another lesson learned – the two aspects of the migrant, embodied in a place of origin, on the one hand, and a new environment, on the other, are subject to multiple stress tests, including the tension between the feeling of belonging 'at home' and the fact of no longer being there. Long after their departure, migrants remain connected to their place of origin, sometimes even more intensely when they are further away, while clinging to the new environment as their last, best hope. Another test is occasioned by the multiple transfers – of news, cultural values, new norms, remittances . . . – between the migrant's point of departure and his point of arrival. The polarity between parents left behind, along with a shared past, and a future that must be built with strangers is frequently short-circuited and can cause violent shocks. Most often, however, ambivalence and indecision prevail: migrants and the relatives who have sent them on their way are playing all the angles to make the best out of the situation, while remaining awash with conflicting feelings and interests. They try to open new doors without closing avenues of retreat. If the migrant finds himself forced to choose, the case of the young South Sudanese rebels that we examined in the previous chapter leads one to think that home is likely to prevail over *hakuma*, the exterior sphere.

When it comes to the crunch, moral security trumps the pursuit of happiness.

Zooming in on the *Mare Nostrum*

In 1957, at the dawn of Africa's independence, the Franco-Tunisian writer Albert Memmi published *The Portrait of the Colonized after the Portrait of the Colonizer* – the French title in translation, which for the English edition published in 1965 became simply *The Colonizer and the Colonized*. The critically acclaimed book, prefaced by Jean-Paul Sartre, explored both perspectives on the key moment of decolonization: the colonial subjects' high hopes for 'liberation' as well as the sullen discon-solation of the empire-builders on their way out. Today, at the dawn of Africa's 'scramble for Europe', a similar double portrait of the protagonists of the coming migratory encounter would be a hazardous enterprise, as the two sides have not yet engaged each other at the predicted scale. But a few things can be said about the African migrants that Europe can expect.

They will be young, that is for sure. And if they practise a reli-gion, they will not do so in private only, or in designated places of worship: their faith will inflect the public sphere in their destina-tion countries. As a result of jihadism, Islam is under close scrutiny across Europe. But the debate aroused in France by the publica-tion in 2017 of Régis Debray's *Le nouveau pouvoir* has drawn attention also to the growing presence of born-again evangelism in Europe (the French, taken unawares by this phenomenon, speak of 'Pentecostal Neo-Protestantism'). Not that evangelical Protestantism – a big tent for a variety of denominations – can be understood as the Christian version of jihadism. But France, the 'eldest daughter of the Church' since Clovis I converted to Catholicism in 496, can be single-minded in religious matters. In French eyes, 'born-again' is easily conflated with 'Americanized'. For this reason the multiplication of Pentecostal churches on French soil is more than a merely spiritual challenge. This is clear from the reaction of Olivier Abel, a professor of Protestant theology at the University of Montpellier. In an opinion piece published in *Le Monde* on 29 August 2017, he identified

> a sort of deep cultural fracture between European Protestantism and an American and globalized Protestantism that comes to us from former colonies, from Africa, Latin America, and soon China. . . . In the near future, Africa will be massively neo-Protestant. Kinshasa – the largest francophone city in the world, larger than Paris – is majority Protestant. The French are unaware of the neo-Protestant demographic bomb that is coming their way. There is an enormous amount of work ahead of us to prepare for a successful acculturation, through public education, music and all the performing arts, but also theology, which had already been discarded [by the French].

Standards of living in Europe and Africa are worlds apart, and so are educational standards. Africa's elite that would be equally considered elite in Europe or America represents a tiny sliver of its population – many of them are Western-educated to begin with, and already live in Western countries to boot. The others – that is, the multitude of sub-Saharan migrants who are likely to arrive over the next decades – will, to European eyes, be rugged, ill-educated and uncompromising people, pioneers who scrabbled over the poverty line in Africa and who seek the kind of work in Europe that will be fully automated by 2050. Many of them will remain poor outsiders in their new home countries, thrown back on a kind of collective endeavour – 'communitarianism', as the French like to say – and a grey economy, in much the same way as European migrants to the eastern seaboard of the United States were upon their arrival from the 1880s onwards. The difference is that labour was at a premium in those days, whereas in the Europe of 2050, gainful work for many sub-Saharan migrants is almost inconceivable without war or a climate catastrophe.

African migrants from south of the Sahara will have learned, precociously, to adapt to adversity as much as to diversity: three-quarters of them do not speak their 'national' language at home due to the ethnic, religious and cultural mosaics cobbled together by their colonizers. It is this daily experience above all that they will be able to share with Europeans in exchange for a piece of the economic pie: their ability to navigate the 'simultaneity of otherwise successive temporalities', their DIY multiculturalism and resourcefulness. That ability has many names in Africa: *jua kali* or 'the hot sun' in Swahili; 'Système D' or 'Article 15' in French-speaking countries; *Kalabule* in Ghana; *Kanju* in Yoruba in southwest Nigeria. Dayo Olopade, a Nigerian raised in the United States, a graduate of Yale University and the author of the 2014 book *The Bright Continent: Breaking Rules and Making Change in Modern Africa*, writes that all these terms boil down to the notion that 'culture is more Darwin than Degas, less about subjective beauty than about practical solutions, and doing much more with far less' (2014: 22). If this were indeed the input brought along by African migrants, that would make the European way of life – based on abundance and, increasingly, the precautionary principle as a default mode – much grittier, for better and for worse. For his part, Jean-François Bayart emphasizes the hardship of the migratory journey to Europe, and believes that 'the difficulties of the trip, which the increase in police controls has made more and more dangerous, has probably forged a new subjectivity: it has become an epic journey, requiring strategies of subterfuge and ruse designed to thwart the calculations of the enemy. It has given birth to a culture of clandestinity, with its own savoir-faire, always free to be used in the future for other ends' (2010: 138–9).

Whether they come with habits acquired 'in-country' or learned the hard way on the road, how can you fault young Africans who are leaving their homes to become 'grown-up', full-fledged adults (Schmitz 2008: 8)? They are taking their chance while they can. Still, in leaving their homelands by any means possible, rather than staying and expressing their dissatisfaction and trying to make things better, they are saying something about their societies that it is important to understand: that they are dysfunctional, and not only in terms of per capita GDP, employment opportunities or a social safety net. They also lack the capacity to generate hope. If, as Pushkin said, 'misfortune is a good school, but happiness is the best university', are African immigrants qualified for life in the West? It seems to me they bring the problems of their own societies, but also the will to solve them in a more enabling environment. As we have already underlined, they are in tune with an American-style modernity whose only enduring tradition is that of radical impermanence. African migrants only bring to Europe what Europe has already bequeathed to the world: 'the malady of infinite aspiration'. The sociologist Émile Durkheim used this phrase to explain the meaning of 'anomie', the term he coined for a lack of shared norms and values within a society, and a breakdown of social bonds caused by the discrepancy between individual actions and normative social standards. When there are too many rival value systems, there is no longer a value system that works for everyone. The 'malady of infinite aspiration' – the frustration born out of boundless desires that can never be fulfilled – captures the dark side of globalization: there are no longer any limits, but there are still borders; the only shared code of conduct is the universal sharing of codes. Historically extraverted, and being 'globalized' rather than 'globalizing' in its own right, Africa more than other parts of the world suffers from exposure to infinite aspiration.

Poverty, in the broader sense of a lack of opportunities and an abundance of missed life chances, is a war of attrition fought every day. The Africans who decide to leave for Europe give up on their homeland. But theirs is a case of escape rather than surrender. Who can number their expectations and illusions, assuming that they converge? I don't exclude the possibility that this 'better life' that migrants so readily invoke may only be, in the words of the French demographer Michèle Tribalat, 'a third-world lifestyle with a European standard of living' (2013: loc. 3139–40). I note at the same time that Yaguine Koita and Fodé Tounkara, the two Guinean boys who froze to death in 1999 in the landing gear of a Brussels-bound airliner, expressed in a letter found on them their desire to learn ('we have too many schools but a tremendous lack of education and instruction'). One way or another, the worst response that one can foist on African migrants is what Hannah Arendt called the 'politics of pity'. But before returning to this in the next chapter – in the context of the 'migratory encounter' in Europe, a century after the 'colonial encounter' in Africa – we need to take a closer look at the 'trial' that African migrants face to reach the Old Continent.

It is important to recall that today's uninvited were yesterday's welcome guests. Until the oil crisis in 1973, European countries signed a sheaf of bilateral agreements to bring in much-needed 'guest workers' – Gastarbeiter in Germany, where the term originated – who helped their economies to prosper. It also bears repeating that, alongside this formal recruitment, sub-Saharan Africans were able to come to Europe without a visa. This was not just a postcolonial entitlement that in France, for example, lasted until 1986, but was also standard practice in other European countries: Senegalese going to Italy did not need a visa until 1990. In retrospect, this laissez-faire policy begs the question whether less surveillance of cross-border movements, despite the risk of abuse, does not promote its own form of self-regulation based on supply and demand in the European labour market and the socio-economic situation at large. Visa restrictions and tighter border controls not only led to a total breakdown of the system in the summer of 2015 but, more importantly, shut the door for migrants who were hoping to return briefly to their home countries but worried that if they did so, they might not get back into Europe. Today, whatever hardships they face in Europe, immigrants are staying put. The solution is certainly not a new open-door policy that would result in the 'invasion' of Europe – the nightmare of populist movements across the continent that are hostile to immigration on principle. But new forms of 'circulatory migration' – based on multiple entry visas or even residence permits granted for two or three years, according to a national quota system that makes the arrival of a new African migrant conditional on the prior departure of a compatriot – could harness the self-regulatory effects of the job market and, even more importantly in my eyes, make the policing of migratory flows a shared responsibility between Europe and Africa. One-for-one migrant substitution – one leaves, another enters – would no longer be the defence of 'Fortress Europe' but the co-management of its drawbridge.

Meanwhile, the Mediterranean remains the proving ground for the relationship between Africa and Europe. For Europeans who can scarcely imagine what living on the equivalent of one or two dollars a day actually means in Africa, there is a *Catch-22* quality to the myriad tracks in the Sahara that lead to the Mediterranean, or *Mare nostrum* as the Romans referred to it. Besides, any journalist who wanted to follow the migrants crossing the desert would be running considerable risks, including being taken hostage by jihadists. The perils for the migrants themselves are difficult to evaluate. The International Organization for Migration estimates that between 1996 and 2013 'at least 1,790 migrants died while trying to cross the Sahara', on average roughly 100 persons each year (IOM 2014: 12). Whatever the true figure – and it strikes me as too low – the criminal logistics of the trans-Saharan migration are rarely brought to the attention of the European public. There are 'hunters' who drive the migrants into 'ghettos', where they wait in makeshift lodgings until it is time to leave; and 'fixers' on mopeds who accompany the convoys like a swarm of mosquitoes, bribing the police at various check-points so the human cargo can pass. In Agadez, Niger's main entry point into the desert, some seventy 'ghettos' form a rather unusual hotel-like infrastructure for an estimated 10,000 migrants a month en route to Libya. In the former country of Gaddafi, the *gidambashi* – or 'credit houses' – serve as retention and torture centres for migrants who have run out of money. Photos or footage of these captives – in a pitiable state, starved and swollen from beatings – are posted on Facebook or sent via WhatsApp to extort ransom from family members to secure their release.[7] As CNN revealed in November 2017, those whose relatives are unable to pay for their freedom are auctioned off on 'slave markets'. Why, given this abuse and the fact that anywhere from 400,000 to 1 million migrants are already stranded in Libya, don't sub-Saharans go through Algeria? 'The route through Arlit [in Niger] into Algeria tends to be used by poorer migrants and is more dangerous than that leading through Libya', according to a 2016 risk analysis by a Euro-African border agency (Frontex 2016: 14). What these even greater perils in Niger and Algeria actually are, and how they can be 'more dangerous' than Libya, is not spelt out in the document.

The Mediterranean has become the media focus of a 'war game', says Harding (2000), among migrants, smugglers, border police and humanitarian agencies. Its legal framework, logistics, security arrangements and politics are constantly shifting. Here are some examples: in 2005, the EU established a Warsaw-based agency known as Frontex, the European Border and Coast Guard Agency, to control its common frontiers. In 2010, a year before his downfall, Gaddafi demanded the EU pay an annual rent of 5 billion euros to prevent migrants from crossing the Mediterranean. Without it, he threatened, 'tomorrow, Europe will no longer be European'. On 18 March 2016, following the record influx of migrants the previous year, the EU agreed to pay Turkey some 6 billion euros in two tranches to close the routes in the Aegean, a move that should keep an estimated 3 million Syrians stranded on Turkish soil. Based on this 'model' of cash for kettling, the EU has, since 2016, negotiated 'immigration conventions' with five African countries – Ethiopia, Nigeria, Niger, Mali and Senegal – to stand to gain from containing would-be migrants in the Horn of Africa and the Sahel. This strategy gets to what Jean-Christophe Rufin – with analytical acumen bordering on clairvoyance – predicted after the fall of the Berlin Wall in his 1991 book *L'Empire et les nouveaux barbares*: the reconstruction of a *limes* – the Roman Empire's border wall – as a means of protecting European civilization. Only this time, it is a wall of money.

There are many ways to keep the messy realities of migration at bay. The photo of the three-year-old Syrian boy, Alan Kurdi – found dead on a Turkish beach on 2 September 2015 after the rubber dinghy his family had boarded to cross the Mediterranean capsized only minutes after pushing back from the shore – left no one untouched. For a moment, it galvanized public sympathy in Europe. But this iconic depiction of loss of life on the way to Europe failed to provide the context of the story it purported to tell – and Europeans were expected to fill in the blanks. Would they have had the same feelings, including a sense of guilt, if they had been told that Alan's family were provisionally resettled in Turkey, where the boy's father held stable employment? Or if they had known that the family was headed to Canada, not Europe, even though their visa application had been turned down by Ottawa? And should we not have picked up from media reports that in the year Alan Kurdi died – 2015, the year of record migration to Europe – the risk of dying for a migrant crossing the Mediterranean was 0.37 per cent? The sums are easy: that year, 1,015,078 migrants reached European shores, while 3,771 others were listed as 'lost at sea or missing'. Here again, it is helpful to contextualize the risk – a calculated risk – that African migrants took in 2015: that year, according to World Bank statistics, the likelihood of dying in childbirth for a woman in South Sudan, the worst place on earth to bring an infant into the world, was 1.7 per cent.[8] In other words, South Sudanese mothers giving birth were four and a half times more likely to die than a migrant crossing the Mediterranean, which has been variously described as an 'open-air cemetery', 'the shame of Europe', even the locus of 'a silent genocide' (Brunel 2014: loc. 2420).

In the absence of familiar benchmarks it is never easy to evaluate an unknown danger, especially not for those who prefer to err on the side of caution when they try to assess the risks Africans take in their daily lives. Were journalists and the public to think twice before they reach for clichés – 'the poorest of the poor braving death' to flee the 'hell' of Africa – a more fact-based discussion of migration would be possible. The tragedy in the Mediterranean was that the humanitarian response to the loss of life inadvertently increased the risk for migrants. According to figures from the IOM, a total of 150,982 migrants crossed the Mediterranean between 1 January and 1 November 2017, while 2,839 others were recorded missing – 2,639 of them on the 'central route' between Libya and Italy that most Africans travel. This meant that, while the global flow of migrants across the Mediterranean had reduced to a number that was sometimes surpassed in a single month in 2015, the likelihood of a migrant perishing had risen to 1.88 per cent – five times higher than it was in the record year of migration to Europe.

How was this possible while all eyes were on the Mediterranean and rescue efforts, quite naturally, had improved since the emergency in 2015? The cruel paradox is that the risk became higher because the humanitarian response became more efficient. Rescue boats were getting closer and closer to Libyan territorial waters, and if there was a danger of drowning, they didn't hesitate to enter to help those in trouble.[9] Smugglers exploited this window by packing growing numbers of migrants onto ever more precarious craft – especially the 9-metre long inflatable boats from China, which at times held up to 130 persons, a number several times their capacity. In exchange for a reduction in the cost of the journey, one of the passengers would be put in charge of 'navigating' and making the emergency call to rescue authorities once the craft reached international waters. To accomplish this, the navigator was provided with a compass and a mobile satellite telephone. In the past, another passenger would also have travelled at a reduced rate by acting as 'Captain', and would be in charge of running the outboard motor. However, as the price of outboard motors began to climb sharply (in the summer of 2017, it was more than 8,000 euros in Libya), ensuring that the motor did not disappear once the rescuers arrived became an issue. The smugglers were then likely to take the motor with them in another boat once the craft carrying the migrants reached the edge of territorial waters, leaving its occupants helpless and adrift – pending the arrival of a rescue ship. In the first six months of 2017, humanitarian aid workers rescued and transported to Italy almost three-quarters of all migrants attempting to cross the Mediterranean – some 93,000 people.[10] In fact, they became so efficient that the smugglers began purchasing even less seaworthy craft than before and an increasing number of Italians and other Europeans started blaming the aid workers for running a kind of Mediterranean Uber, on call to ferry new migrants to Europe.

Since the summer of 2017, the situation in the Mediterranean has again shifted. The 'humanitarian trap' that incentivized smugglers to lower their already minimal security standards, luring migrants onto floating devices rather than navigable boats, has been largely dismantled. Even before the ascent to power of an anti-immigration coalition in Rome in 2018, Italy had struck a deal with Libyan warlords and equipped the country's coast guard, in a bid to curb the rate of migrant departures. Since then, the new government has prohibited humanitarian rescue ships from entering Italian ports. Meanwhile, tens of thousands of migrants, who have not obtained asylum in Europe since they arrived in 2015, are wandering the continent in search of a host country. Technically referred to as 'secondary admissions', they have become a pariah class of persons for EU countries trying to foist them off on their neighbours. The twists and turns of this unfolding news story are crucial to the future of Europe and Africa. They also tell us, as I have argued throughout this book, that neither Europe nor Africa has yet taken the full measure of the challenge that lies ahead. The two continents are still unprepared for a migratory encounter of unprecedented magnitude.

5

Europe as Destination and Destiny

For a critical mass of Africans, living conditions will soon be defined more by corrosive frustration than uncompromising misery, and their continent will be transformed into a departure hall. When 'the first glimmerings of prosperity' shine with more intensity, how many Africans will leave for Europe? Some 150 million, if Africa follows the example of Mexico after it emerged from absolute poverty in the mid-1970s. But that figure provides us only with an order of magnitude derived from a historical precedent. For now, in fact, the only certainty is that a large-scale 'migratory encounter' is set to occur in the near future between Africa and Europe. How large will depend on the circumstances and, to a great extent, on Europe's wager on 'diversity', a shibboleth in the original sense of the word – a watchword separating friend from foe – that we will examine in more detail. The term is divisive: opponents of diversity are often accused of xenophobia and even racism, while its supporters are often suspected of wanting to dilute national identity or, for those who bristle at the very term, to weaken 'that which holds together the citizens of a state'. If there are only rights and duties between parties to a bargain, nationality becomes as transactional as any service agreement.

African migration resembles a fountain with multiple over-flow basins. So vigorous is its demographic growth that the rural exodus has washed hundreds of millions of people into the cities without emptying the villages. Many villagers have moved to big cities or their national capital, while others have crossed the border to settle in a neighbouring country, often in a regional metropolis. Finally, with the 'help' of smugglers and traffickers, an increasing number of migrants leave the continent and head to Europe (though not exclusively). There, assuming they find a job, they provide European economies with the brains or brawn in demand, and ageing societies with the youth and diversity many politicians and experts hail as a demographic boon. In their view, Young Africa and the Old Continent are destined to be partners: Africa's youth bulge will compensate for the pensioners' bulge in Europe. Put more cynically, they see Africans as 'retirement fodder' and believe that, in exchange, Europe will offer Young Africa a spillway for its many 'failed adults'.

Should African migrants be allowed to enter Europe in large numbers? Or should they be stopped at the borders, or at least – *horresco referens* – filtered by aptitude and 'profiled'? Can the Old Continent survive the looming bankruptcy of its contributory pension schemes that are based on intergenerational solidarity? Or should it accept that to finance even a minimum of its social security needs, a quarter of its under-thirties could be 'African' in 2050?[1] The immigration debate has always been a virulent one, and it risks becoming even more so in the future. Every word counts as much for its subtext as its explicit meaning. Hence the frequent impugning of motives and use of prosecutorial language. In Europe, one side is afraid of losing its soul while the other is intent on proving it has one. Only on rare occasions is their feud interrupted by an effusion of empathy. This was the case in May 2018 when a twenty-two-year-old illegal Malian immigrant, Mamoudou Gassama, rescued a four-year-old boy dangling from a balcony in Paris.[2] Apparently oblivious to danger, Gassama scaled five storeys of a building to whisk the toddler to safety. Caught on a mobile phone video, the incident went viral. Gassama was invited to the Élysée to meet with President Macron, who offered him French citizenship and a job in the Paris fire service.

In this chapter, as a corrective to the ebb and flow of soul-searching, I want to 'de-moralize' the debate on African migration to Europe. I mean this literally. While there are obviously important ethical implications, the decision for or against a migratory policy is not a choice between Good and Evil. In European democracies, it is about first deliberating and then agreeing on the rules for the admission of third-country nationals to EU territory. These rules ought to be in the best – not the basest or the most self-sacrificing – interests of its citizenry. It is a question of good governance, not of heaven or hell on earth.

Human migration is as old as humanity, and likely to last as long. But its intensification between Africa and Europe requires both sides to reframe the migration debate in order to build the broadest political consensus possible. For this to happen, Africa needs to realize that the massive departure of its most dynamic citizens – often its best-educated – represents a net loss for the continent. And Europe must take the full measure of the migratory pressure that Africa will bring to bear on its territory and address three core questions: which migrants should be welcomed, how many, and according to what criteria?

Two principles might guide this debate. On the one hand, Europe must abide by the numerous international treaties on rights and duties to which its member states are signatories: many of these treaties originated in Europe, when the continent thought of itself – for better or worse – as a paragon of civilization. On the other hand, Europe should not consider 'the' African migrant and potential fellow citizen as someone who stands vaguely for an abstract humanity. Africans arriving at Europe's borders are distinct and distinctive: men, women and children who come from different parts of a continent almost seven times the size of Western Europe. They speak their own languages and bring with them cultural traditions, norms and values that it is not inappropriate for their hosts to examine before extending their hospitality. In short, when trying to formulate a 'good' immigration policy, irenic universalism inspired by a vague brotherhood of men is as prejudicial as nationalistic or nativist egoism, or any cult of blood and soil.

Don't Reckon Without Your Host

A massive repopulation of the world is underway, and we are all part of it. Either we are settling in a new country or we are on the receiving end as hosts – a word that shares etymological roots with both 'hospitality' and 'hostility'. Migrants are the pioneers of a new life elsewhere. They leave one place and move to a more promising one, on a legal journey with official paperwork or a clandestine odyssey. Earlier, we distinguished between an active and a passive role in globalization. But that is not exactly right. Both the 'globalizer' and the 'globalized' have agency, or at least some capacity to change the course of events, even if that capacity is not the same in both cases. For example, Africans have discovered ingenious uses for mobile phones. But they haven't yet acquired the means to produce this technology, which is imported and essentially developed outside the continent. One could perhaps talk about the 'strategic' agency of globalizers and the 'tactical' agency of the globalized. In any event, the ability to act is unequally distributed across the world, just as wealth is.

Another inequality is linked to the distribution of 'world time', the French historian Fernand Braudel's *'temps du monde'*: time, that is to say, as it is lived and apprehended at the cutting edge of innovation and accumulation. In a globalized world, societies at the forefront of modernity no longer have the monopoly on 'world time' but they are still hoarding it. Europeans live in it, while African migrants come from time zones that, as we have seen, are characterized by the simultaneity of epochs that elsewhere – namely in Europe – have been successive. When both meet in the 'migratory encounter', the African migrant as well as the European need to agree on the same time and set their watches accordingly. Both must make an effort, but it is not the same effort. On his way to Europe, the African has crossed not only space, but time as well. The European hosts, for their part, must get used to the different temporality which the migrant has introduced into their everyday environment, and which reminds them of their own past. But what the African brings to this encounter is not precisely the European past. It differs slightly or considerably, and these minor or major differences trouble the host (and if Freud's 'narcissism of minor differences' is a valid idea, the small discrepancies might be even more troublesome than the stark differences). In any event, the hosts' quality of life is changed, because more and more foreigners – strangers, indeed – have become their neighbours. Some of them – usually in the poor neighbourhoods that are mostly affected – might inveigh against having been 'invaded'.

Anthropologists have reflected on 'stranger-host relationships' in societies all over the world: the arrival of foreigners can be destabilizing, their presence unsettling. Pretending otherwise is surely disingenuous in view of the 'lengthy process of welcoming and aiding and what that means as a matter of work for oneself and others', something the Algerian writer Kamel Daoud has spoken of while warning against 'an angelic attitude that will ultimately kill'.[3] Neither the stranger nor the host are a priori 'good' or 'evil', 'generous' or 'selfish'. Both find themselves in a situation where they need to understand the different circumstances that have brought them together. To my mind, the assumption that 'the other is myself in other circumstances' is a good starting point for finding common ground. In any event, except for the duty to rescue that applies to asylum seekers (and is limited by the principle that they should not constitute a criminal threat to the community), indifference is neither wrong nor immoral (Wellman and Cole 2011: 36–7). Indeed, to be meaningful, as Washington University philosopher Christopher Heath Wellman argues in *Debating the Ethics of Immigration: Is There a Right to Exclude?*, freedom of association must also imply the freedom *not* to associate. As for the impetus to help poor countries, the question is – and we will look into this in a moment – whether the inequalities of the world can best be overcome by welcoming migrants from the South. Whatever the response, a concern for greater international equality should not be confused with a vision of open borders as the royal road to achieving that goal. It is not inconsistent to favour worldwide social justice and oppose the free movement of persons.

'He that reckons without his host must reckon again' – this saying, which refers to the innkeeper as the definitive authority when the bill is drawn up, holds good for immigration as well. So let us take as a given, and not as a genuflexion before the altar of autochthony, that the host is an entitled figure on home turf. Otherwise, the concepts of sovereignty and nationality would no longer mean anything. One might wish for, or even predict, the obsolescence of borders and nationalities. However, for now, the passport remains the membership card for a national 'club' that provides certain rights in exchange for certain obligations. How exactly a national community defines itself – through a blood pact or a social contract freely consented to, with or without a state religion, etc. – matters very little in this context. That is because no one can dictate to a community how it must define the commonality of its members, especially not those who are applying for membership. One doesn't join a club by relaxing the rules. These can be renegotiated, but only after one has become a member. Of course, there are extreme and painful examples of the will to exclude. In an attempt to 'purge' history of any extraneous influences, the French nationalist Maurice Barrès asserted in his 1888 book *Under the Eyes of the Barbarians*: 'I defend my cemetery. I have abandoned all other positions.' Faced with such emphatic rejection, we have no choice but to let the beleaguered ego dig its own grave.

Dayo Olopade thinks that 'today, African diaspora maps are reverse models of colonialism' (2014: 83). It is clear what Olopade means to say. But this is to overlook the slave trades and their consequences, above all the emergence of the Black Atlantic: Brazil, for example, is hardly a 'reverse model of colonialism'. More importantly, Olopade turns 'postcoloniality' into an open-ended category. Yet colonialism lasted only about eighty years south of the Sahara. The 'colonial imprint' cannot overwrite the longer history of the continent before and since colonialism. As we have seen, a certain familiarity links Nigerians and South Africans with the UK, Senegalese and Central Africans with France, Angolans and Mozambicans with Portugal, or the Congolese of the DRC with Belgium (known as *lola*, or 'heaven', in Lingala, a Congolese lingua franca). But during the sixty years since their independence, many former colonies have redirected their antennae. Kinshasa has turned towards France and the United States, while Kigali has had two successive re-orientations away from Belgium: first to France and then to Washington and London, which also included changing its official language to English in only two years, beginning in 2008. And looking beyond Africa, why would you expect Vietnam, for instance, to consider the Eiffel Tower the umbilical centre of the world just because it was once a French colony?

France, the Western power most closely and durably involved in sub-Saharan affairs, is an interesting case. Its colonial policy of 'assimilation' fostered elite connivance between Paris and the various capitals of francophone Africa. The French decolonized under the motto 'leaving, all the better to remain' – '*partir pour mieux rester*' – and maintained a tutelary presence in Africa until the end of the Cold War, during which the 'gendarme of Africa' was mandated by the West with keeping order in the French-speaking parts of the continent. Bereft of this geopolitical rationale after the end of the East-West confrontation, the *France-Afrique* dyad gained dubious notoriety as *Françafrique* or *France à fric* – a truncation as well as a pun on 'corrupt France' – a

Franco-African mafia that many believe is still running the show, pulling strings behind the scenes. Yet the migratory magnetism France exerts on its former possessions south of the Sahara has lost much of its power. Francophone Africans increasingly migrate to Germany, the UK and the Nordic countries. I see three reasons for this. First, as already mentioned, members of the African elite shun France precisely because of its postcolonial meddling in the affairs of their home countries. Secondly, *Françafrique* is no longer an accurate description of the Franco-African relationship: since the mid-1990s, France's presence and leverage south of the Sahara have greatly diminished. However, the pretence of a 'deep' Franco-African state continues to reassure both sides about their enduring relevance for each other – albeit now mostly as partners in backdoor dealings. Thirdly and most importantly, the Franco-African subcontinent has disintegrated under the pounding surf and backwash of younger generations south of the Sahara. Today, sub-Saharan migrants seek opportunities anywhere in the world, and not only in their erstwhile colonial metropoles. Genoa, Italy, has become more 'African' than many French or British port cities; the percentage of African students is higher in Montreal than in Paris or London; many Sudanese have settled in Atlanta, under the illuminated signs of CNN and Coca-Cola; thousands of Eritreans and Ethiopians call Washington DC home. In the game of intercontinental musical chairs, 'postcoloniality' is a fusty melody, less and less audible over the blare of newer and catchier tunes. If the colonial connection continues to play at all, it is due to the diasporas, their longstanding trail back to their ex-metropoles and their enduring role as a welcome-desk for compatriots leaving home. This chain migration sometimes nurtures the fantasy of a resentful Africa imposing a 'revenge colonization' on Europe. Seen from the shorelines at their points of departure, Lobo Antunes's returning caravels are easily confused with warships.

'We were in the heart of Africa / Jealous guardians of our colours / When, under a magnificent sun / Resounded this victory cry: / Forward! Forward! Forward!' The song is still widely known in France, where it is part of the national repertoire of military marches and in the French army's official songbook. When the Malian army was invited to march down the Champs-Élysées in the 2013 Bastille Day festivities, that is what it played. And at least older generations in France would recognize the chorus: 'We are the Africans / Who return from afar / We come from the colonies / To save the country', or, in one version, 'To defend the country'. With this 'Song of the Africans' on their lips, the French Army B, commanded by General Jean de Lattre de Tassigny, fought alongside the 7th US Army when they landed in Provence on 15 August 1944. Half of these 'French' troops were African colonial subjects, in particular North Africans, the other half European settlers in Africa and, again, especially in North Africa. Ironically, the operation's code name – Anvil, and later Operation Dragoon – accurately reflected the situation of all these Africans, white, black and brown: they were caught between a hammer and an anvil, just as the German army was caught by the Allies' double landing in Normandy and Provence; and the Africans setting foot on the Mediterranean beaches were sometimes as 'dragooned' as Winston Churchill felt at the time. He had wanted to engage the German army in central Europe in order to arrive in Berlin before the Soviet forces, but had been overruled. So Churchill insisted that the name of the landing alluded to the fact that his hand had been forced.

The *Mare nostrum*, which is shared by Africa, Europe and the Middle East, is not only the cradle of ancient civilizations, and today a body of water crossed by migrants in makeshift craft. It is a sea where phantom boats from various collective imaginations prefer to anchor, like those conjured up by the French writer Jean Raspail. He predicted in 1973 – the year of the first oil shock that put an abrupt end to the three decades of postwar European prosperity – that a million of the world's destitute would invade France and run Western civilization aground. In his work of fiction, *The Camp of the Saints*, which is awash with references to the

Apocalypse of St John, Raspail forecast that these 'hordes' of poor people, whom he depicted as utterly repugnant, would storm the same beaches between Nice and Toulon where in 1944 colonized Africans had landed to liberate 'their' metropole. 'What if *they* were to come? I did not know who "they" were, but it seemed inevitable to me that the numberless disinherited people of the South would, like a tidal wave, set sail one day for this opulent shore, our fortunate country's wide-gaping frontier', Raspail explained in 2011 in the foreword to the fourth edition of his book. I don't mention it here to reignite a controversy that has regularly flared up since its publication and at each republication – many have rejected *The Camp of the Saints* as a 'racist tract', while others have praised its 'prophetic nature', especially after a million migrants crossed the Mediterranean in 2015. In the end there is only a superficial resemblance between the arrival of the 2015 migrants – for the most part war refugees from Syria, Afghanistan and Iraq – and Raspail's lurid prognostications. Still, they seem to me 'revelatory' in much the same way as *Submission* – Michel Houellebecq's 2015 narrative of the ascent to power of 'moderate' Islamists in France – which tracks the European fantasy of Muslim conquest. In both cases, historical revisionism is conjugated in the future perfect tense to cast dark shadows on Europe's present: the reader is plunged into a world where Charles Martel will have been roundly defeated in the battle of Tours, where Europe, assailed by Attila and his Huns, will have been trounced in the Catalaunian plains . . .

Plugging a Leaky Dike with Sandbags of Euros

Europe in 1850 – not counting Russia – had some 200 million inhabitants. By 1914, at the beginning of the First World War, it had gained around 100 million more. The two dates bookmark the beginning and end of Europe's demographic transition. During this time, almost 60 million Europeans left the continent: 43 million for the United States, 11 million for Latin America, 3.5

million for Australia and 1 million for South Africa. Then, after the Second World War, there was a massive movement north from southern Europe, such that today in France there are some 3.5 million first or second-generation Portuguese, Italian and Spanish. The question is why Africa would not be next, why it, too, would not have the 'right' to regulate its own demographic pressure by opening a migratory escape valve. Isn't Europe, which was able to foist its own surplus population on the rest of the world, hypocritical when it refuses to accept today what it practised itself in the past?

In the world as it is today, there is no absolute 'right' to live where one wants. That free choice is denied by the sovereign right of states – and not only the rich and powerful states – to regulate access to their territory. Besides, immigrants themselves are sometimes tempted to shut the door behind them, once they arrive: few feel under an obligation to share their newfound prosperity with latecomers.[4] The claim that there should be a universal right to come and go freely, and to settle in any other country, is sometimes made with reference to 'the free circulation of goods and capital', one of the catchphrases of globalization. But that too is a specious argument. Just try sending a package or money order abroad, acts which are the apex of regulatory overkill on both the sending and receiving end. More important, while it may not be fair that different parts of the world face their migratory challenge in more or less favourable circumstances, it is also the case that countries today are not allowed to pollute as blithely as the pioneering nations of industrialization. Africa can jump directly to mobile telephony, skipping the expensive, hard-wired copper lines the developed countries had to put into place. Is it fair that their predecessors had to pay for the installation of such costly infrastructure? Or that Africans today, as former Ivorian president Laurent Gbagbo once explained to me, must 'fight their French Revolution under the eye of Amnesty International', a constraint that did not exist in 1789? Fair or unfair, Africa will have to complete its demographic transition in a far more bounded and scrutinized world than before. And the continent has only itself to blame for its pertinacious indifference to large-scale family planning. National campaigns to promote birth control, as in Bangladesh ('A Small Family is a Happy Family') or Jamaica ('Two is Better than Too Many'), have barely been tried in any country south of the Sahara.

Well before the record migratory influx of 2015, the EU had already begun to doubt its ability to close off its borders to migrants from the South. It had tested an uncompromising response in a very limited area, around Ceuta and Melilla, the two tiny Spanish enclaves on the northern shore of Morocco's Mediterranean coast. Both were entirely ringed by steel fences which year after year grew higher and higher – currently they top 7 metres. Since 2006, images of migrants clutching these fences in a last-ditch effort to enter 'Fortress Europe' have evoked memories of the despised Iron Curtain that ran across Europe until 1989. With that disfiguring injury healed, how can Europe fence itself off from 'the wretched of the earth', as Frantz Fanon called the people of the Global South? Both really and figuratively, the 'escalation' around Ceuta and Melilla became an incalculable hazard. In February 2014, to prevent the most audacious migrants from simply swimming around the fence, the Spanish coast guard fired rubber bullets at the heads bobbing in the water. At least fifteen people died.[5] Europe's doubts about the feasibility of sealing its borders are sustained by moral qualms as well as a sober cost-benefit analysis: an incessant search for clandestine migrants in the twenty-six Schengen-area countries, the permanent detention of some 140,000 people awaiting trial, the right to appeal in case their claim is rejected, a chartered flight home – all very expensive undertakings. According to its National Audit Office, Great Britain alone would have to spend 9 billion euros to repatriate all of its illegal immigrants in a process that would last anywhere from fifteen to thirty years (Harding 2012: loc. 1189–92). By comparison, the total of 6 billion euros paid to Turkey in 2016 and 2018 to prevent some 3 million migrants from reaching

European soil seems like a good deal, a bargain price in fact, especially given that there is no bad press for human rights violations (there are few NGO witnesses in Turkey to report them).

Since 2015, the EU has redoubled its efforts to subsidize the various national police forces in countries to the south and east of its common borders. It does not seem to matter who its partners are in this effort, from Turkish president Recep Tayyip Erdoğan to the militias of Libya: Turkey signed up to the 1951 Refugee Convention with a proviso that it would only obtain for those seeking asylum in Europe; Libya has never signed. In a September 2017 interview in *Le Monde*, Joanne Liu, the president of MSF International (the umbrella organization of Médecins sans frontières), said the situation in Libya was the result of

> a collection of different things: the departure of Gaddafi, the coexistence of three governments, the proliferation of militias, the absence of any rule of law . . . All this has led to a vast system of predatory behaviour aimed at the most desperate people. With its current policies the EU . . . is helping support this criminal enterprise. Take the budget adopted by the EU. More than 90 million euros were approved in April to help Libya deal with its migratory problems. But we know there is no oversight to safeguard how this money is spent. At the end of July, 46 million euros were disbursed to create a Libyan coast guard. Yet they are trained to bring migrants back to Libya, into this abject environment.[6]

At first glance, Europe's strategy – to plug a leaky dike with sandbags full of euros and stem the migratory tide – seems as different from that of the United States as an ATM is from a military base. America has in effect opted for the militarization of its 3,145 kilometre border with Mexico, whose 350 million legal crossings a year make it the most frequently traversed frontier in the world. This decision occurred well before the 2016 election of Donald Trump, who upped the bidding and threw several gratuitous insults of Mexicans – 'drug users', 'criminals', 'rapists' – into the bargain.[7] After the passage of the 2006 Secure Fence Act, former president George W. Bush spent 1.75 billion dollars to build a combination of vehicle barriers and pedestrian fencing along a nearly 1,000 kilometre stretch of border. In 2010, when this approach was dropped because of its exorbitant cost, President Barack Obama invested a further 600 million dollars to hire more surveillance personnel, increasing the number of border patrol agents to a record high of 20,000. In addition, a federal programme, Operation Streamline, began in 2005. It adopted a zero-tolerance approach to unauthorized border crossings, trying people en masse. Ninety-nine per cent of those arrested have been convicted, and most of them subsequently deported. The usefulness of this panoply of repressive measures is not clear. According to US Department of Homeland Security statistics, of the 200,000 illegal immigrants who cross the border each year, fewer than half, around 85,000, remain in the United States. The rest return to Mexico, as no doubt an even larger number of their illegal compatriots residing in the United States – 5.8 million in 2016, a number that has been shrinking for the past ten years – would also do if their route home was not blocked by ever more complex obstacles. In fairness, what is true for Mexico is not true for all of Latin America and, in particular, the states of Central America, whose inhabitants still leave in large numbers. But the lack of a reliable social safety net in the United States tends to keep the number of illegal immigrants without work or a family network in check, simply because it is difficult to survive without them. That is not the case in the European Union, whose 7 per cent of the world population accounts for half of the social welfare money invested globally. A well-cosseted exception in an otherwise more exposed world, the EU is very attractive – and difficult to protect. Its land border stretches 9,000 kilometres and its coastline runs 42,000 kilometres – more than the circumference of the earth at the equator. However, European and American strategies to block immigration are not, after all, that different:

in paying states on its border areas to serve as detention camps, Europe is trying to shelter itself behind a wall of money; Donald Trump wants to build a physical barrier on the border from sea to shining sea and then send Mexico the bill.

'Bowling Alone'

There used to be a strong family resemblance between the New World and the Old Continent. It dated back to a time when almost every European had an 'uncle' in America. But that was before the abolition of nationality-based immigration quotas in 1965, when nine out of ten new arrivals in the United States came from Europe – a proportion that has since then been inverted. Besides, the family resemblance masked profound cultural differences. Take, for example, a key moment in *The Great Gatsby*, when the hero says: 'Can't repeat the past? . . . Why of course you can!' For generations of young Americans, the words of F. Scott Fitzgerald's protagonist meant that Gatsby was irredeemably lost. By contrast, European readers would not linger over such a mundane statement of truth: for them, the past is always ready to reappear at the threshold of the future. Only Americans have completely internalized 'creative destruction' as the sine qua non of progress.

We err on the side of platitude when we repeat that the United States is a nation of immigrants. But they are never the same immigrants. The US, which today represents less than 5 per cent of the world's population, is now home to four times more immigrants than any other country (Taylor 2014: loc. 786–9).[8] Everything is arranged for the new arrivals, from the 'welcome wagon' – carrying information and gifts from local merchants for new residents in an area – to the path towards naturalization, with stops for ESL (English as a Second Language) classes in every school. Which is not to say that Trump is the first politician to break with this tradition of open arms. To give just one example, Thomas Watson, the Georgia populist elected first to the House of Representatives and then the Senate, wrote in 1910 that 'the scum of creation has been dumped on us. Some of our principal cities are more foreign than American. The most dangerous and corrupting hordes of the Old World have invaded us' (Taylor 2014: loc. 2012–14). Watson was then targeting Jews and Catholics, Poles, Italians and other European immigrants, including those whom the country's WASPs (White Anglo-Saxon Protestants) viewed as too 'swarthy'. This was long before the WASP establishment agreed to a racially expanded version of whites, the so-called 'Caucasians'. It was a fantastical typology to begin with, one based on a description of one single cranium, but it ensured that whites would maintain their numerical superiority throughout the twentieth century. The white-skinned ascendancy was also averse to 'Orientals': until 1952, foreign-born Asians – then the main underqualified and overexploited immigrant labour force in America – could not become US citizens.

1965 was a turning point, not only for African Americans and their civil rights, but – and this is not simply a coincidence – for all people of colour coming to the United States. Standing at the foot of the Statue of Liberty, President Lyndon Johnson signed the Immigration and Nationality Act of 1965, which ended restrictions on the entry of non-Europeans to America, abolishing nationality-based selection and replacing it with an entry system focusing on job skills and family reunification. Since then, some 60 million new immigrants have made the United States their second home (some 78 million when one includes unauthorized immigrants and their children already there). Three-quarters of them have come from South America and Asia. Today, 'Asian-Americans' represent 6.4 per cent of the population, with the most mixed marriages of any ethnic group. They are today the best educated and the most prosperous of any migrant intake, with a household income in 2015 that was 25 per cent higher than that of white Americans. Immigration to the US from Africa became statistically significant only towards the end of the twentieth century. According to a 2017 study by the Pew Research Center, the number of Africans in the United States has grown from 80,000 in 1970 to 881,000 in 2000 to 2.1 million in 2015.[9] That year, the self-declared African diaspora in the US (including children and grandchildren) comprised 3.3 million people, slightly above 1 per cent of the total population. Since 2010, African immigration to the US has grown faster than any other migrant intake.[10] In 2016, Africans represented 37 per cent of all asylum seekers. Overall, their educational achievement is superior to the US average but varies considerably, between Egyptians and Nigerians at the upper end and Liberians and Somalis at the lower end. Despite highly visible individual success stories in science, arts, entertainment and sports, sub-Saharan Africans were slightly more likely in 2015 to live in poverty (19 per cent) than all immigrants (17 per cent) or the US-born (14 per cent). The highest poverty rates affected Somalis (46 per cent) and Liberians (22 per cent).[11]

The basic factsheet of the *new* United States, immigration-wise, can be summed up in a few sentences. Each year about 4 million Americans are born, 2.5 million die, and another 1 million are added through immigration. Since 2008, a majority of those immigrants have been Asian, although Latinos – Mexicans in particular – still represent the largest percentage of the immigrant stock, which has now begun to age; their inflow has been declining since 2005, while immigration from Africa, rising from low levels, has increased by 71 per cent since 2010. Even among illegal immigrants, two-thirds have been living in the United States for more than ten years. But what is far more difficult to summarize are the actual characteristics of American society after two centuries of immigration. Currently, the country's immigration profile looks like an hour-glass, broad at both the bottom with low-skilled labourers and the top with highly educated immigrants from around the world – but narrow in the middle. Most experts agree that foreign labour tends to depress salaries in certain sectors of the economy, especially seasonal agricultural work, fast food and other low-wage parts of the service sector. They further agree that the world's best and brightest who have settled in America – including from Africa, among them a Nobel Prize laureate in chemistry, the Egyptian Ahmed Zewail, and numerous full tenured professors at Ivy League universities – have helped make the US economy one of constant renewal and innovation. Since 1990 and the beginnings of the digital revolution, a quarter of the fastest-growing US companies have been founded by immigrants. But when it comes to defining the new paradigm of living together, there is little consensus, even if most experts agree that the melting-pot theory of assimilation is outdated, and that the country's future will be defined by a multi-ethnic and multicultural mosaic instead. One of the best indicators of this trend is the low rate of naturalization among new immigrants in the United States, which hovers at around 50 per cent, far less than in Western Europe and not even remotely close to naturalization rates in Canada or Australia. More and more foreigners are coming to the United States simply because it offers more job opportunities than their country of origin, rather than to take part in its unique social experiment which combines openness to the rest of the world with a strong national identity and an unshakeable faith in American 'exceptionalism'. Is this a reflection of the US becoming less exceptional as other countries follow its example or, just the opposite, of the 'American model' running out of steam?

In his bestselling book *Bowling Alone: The Collapse and Revival of American Community*,[12] Harvard political scientist Robert Putnam argues, using a raft of statistics, that 'social capital' in the United States has been in free fall since the 1960s.[13] According to him, social capital is made up of 'bonding capital' that links us to others by natural resemblance, shared culture or station in life, and 'bridging capital' that allows us to connect with people for whom this is a priori not the case. Put simply, Putnam posits that the more comfortable one feels in one's own culture, and with one's social equals, the easier it is to be open to foreigners and different ways of life. Without a safe and stable spot from which bridges to otherness can be built, a 'hunkering down' attitude sets in, and not just towards less familiar members of society but towards society as a whole. It is as if interpersonal trust suddenly evaporates.

The antithesis of the United States is Japan, for two centuries – until 1854 – a 'closed' country.[14] On the American side, *E pluribus unum*, 'Out of many, one'; on the Japanese, a premium laid on national cohesion and ethnic and cultural uniformity. In 2015, only 1.5 per cent of the Japanese population had been born in another country compared with 13.3 per cent in America. That same year, refugee status was granted to just twenty-seven people in Japan, even though the country is the fourth largest donor to the United Nations High Commissioner for Refugees.[15] In 2017, the African diaspora in Japan accounted for 0.01 per cent of the total population.[16] In public debate and opinion polls, immigration remains anathema, except in the limited case of nursing assistants from Vietnam, Indonesia or the Philippines (although replacing them with robots is a priority of the Japanese hi-tech industry). And all this despite a litany of reasons that elsewhere would justify a massive intake of foreigners to increase and rejuvenate the country's population: Japan's fertility rate descended in 2005 to 1.26 children for each woman of child-bearing age (well below the population replacement rate of 2.1), and the Japanese population was projected to fall from 128 million people to 87 million in 2060 (in which case, in a little less than forty years, four Japanese out of every ten would be more than sixty-five years old). Already, by 2050, a hundred working adults in Japan are expected to contribute for ninety-six non-working people – seventy-two retirees and twenty-four children. By comparison, in the United States, a hundred working adults will have to support only seventy-four dependants, half retirees and half children.

Japan appears to confirm that bonding capital – emotional attachments between similar people – suffers when there is a shortage of bridging capital – the ability to reach out to people who are a priori different.[17] It should be no surprise that hope, *kibo*, is a rare commodity in a society with a rapidly ageing population and an economy that has suffered for decades from stagflation. But in Japan, the phenomenon of young people who lock themselves in the darkness of their rooms, only opening the door for their meal tray, and who rarely communicate through more than a cyber-connected, pixelated screen, has become sufficiently widespread to have been given its own name, *hikkimori*, or 'social recluses'. Japanese society is top-heavy. Its pensioners are privileged because of the former norm of a 'job for life', and their growing numbers mean they are the most courted electorate. These elderly loom large over a youthful demographic of whom 38 per cent lack any job stability. Almost one-third of all Japanese – 31 per cent – live alone. If one had to characterize contemporary Japan in only two phrases, they would be *ohitorisama*, 'doing things alone', and *muen shakai*, a 'no relationship society'. It is *Bowling Alone* all over again.

Smashing the Actuarial Tables

The United States and Japan provide reference points to 'de-provincialize' the European case. In 1900, one quarter of the world's population was European; today, Europeans make up 7 per cent; in 2050, they will account for 4.5 per cent of the global population, and nearly one-third of them will be more than sixty-five years old. By then, the Old Continent will be an apt demographic description. In Europe, the ratio between working adults making contributions to the state and the young people and old people who benefit from those payments is deteriorating rapidly. This has major implications for a social security system based on inter-generational solidarity. If Europe follows its current trajectory, its dependency ratio will have climbed between 2000 and 2050 from four active workers for one dependant to only two active workers per dependant. By contrast, south of the Sahara, this ratio will steadily improve, at least on paper. For example, Niger will have nineteen working-age adults for one dependant in 2050, and enjoy an incredible 'demographic dividend' assuming there is full employment. Yet, as we have seen, there is an enormous gap, an abyss, really, between the number of positions on the Nigerian employment market and the number of job seekers. Currently, sub-Saharan Africa as a whole would have to create 22 million jobs each year in order to provide work for the job seekers coming onto the market. The region is so far from reaching that goal that, by comparison, Europe's shores seem much more attainable.

Demographers are their society's actuaries – experts who compute health hazards, accidents and natural catastrophes into a global risk assessment for insurance companies. They are diviners who, instead of throwing bones, spread data on sheets. Like all prophets, they wrestle with what they foresee, wavering between the satisfaction of being proven right and the dread inspired by a fate they would want to avert. The latter was the case for the father of modern demography in France, Alfred Sauvy, in a study released in 1946 in which he assessed France's immigration needs. If the country were to reach a 'structural equilibrium' between workers and dependants, he argued, France would urgently need to add some 5.3 million people to its population – a 13 per cent increase in a country with 40 million inhabitants at the time. Sauvy, who died in 1990, did not live to see France achieve this 'ideal' level of immigration, which was attained in 2005. Which is to say, a certain prudence is in order when dealing with the meretricious eloquence of numbers. What of the prospect that Africa will see its number of working-age people quintuple over the next forty years while Europe's will diminish over the same period by one-third? Laying out the issue in such an obliging way suggests that the demographic asymmetry between the two continents is actually an opportunity – that the two problems can be folded into a single elegant solution.

On the European level, a scenario known as 'Convergence' was outlined by EU demographers for the period 2010–2060. Convergence aims to make up for an anticipated decline of the European population by some 70 million over the next half century, and bring that figure up to 517 million in 2060, from 501 million in 2010. To pull this off, the plan calls for the EU to absorb 86 million migrants, or 1.72 million each year, a number significantly higher than the record total of migrants – 1.256 million – who arrived in 2015. What that would mean on a human level for both the migrants and those who are supposed to welcome them is not discussed in the study. Its sole preoccupation is Europe's depopulation, specifically in Germany, Italy and Spain, which are expected to lose, respectively, 24 million, 15 million and 8 million inhabitants, or 29 per cent, 25 per cent and 18 per cent of their populations as they stood in 2010. The only remedy suggested by the study is more immigration. Logically, these migrants would come from Africa, the world's most dynamic demographic region and Europe's neighbour.

UN demographers also outlined several hypothetical scenarios in a 2000 study entitled 'Replacement Migration: Is it a Solution to Declining and Ageing Populations?'[18] They could not possibly have known that Renaud Camus, the French writer who believes that Muslim migrants are about to colonize France, would call his 2011 book on the subject *The Great Replacement*. Unlike Camus, the UN demographers were not interested in identity politics but in data-based projections of the world's demographic future. They calculated that, if the EU simply wanted to maintain the population it had in 1995, relying only on immigration, it would have to welcome 949,000 immigrants on average per year through to 2050, about 100,000 more per year than over the course of the 1990s, when immigration averaged 857,000 per year. To stabilize its *working-age* population, it would have to admit 1.6 million foreigners each year, almost double the intake during the 1990s (and 400,000 more migrants than arrived in Europe in 2015). According to the study, that would result in a European Union whose population would be three-quarters foreigners or the children of foreigners by 2050. Finally, if the EU wanted to maintain the same *ratio* it had in 1990 between active workers and dependants, 14 million immigrants would have to be admitted each year. 'This scenario is clearly not realistic; therefore, immigration cannot prevent ageing of the population', the UN demographers concluded. They went on to consider other variables besides immigration, such as the age of retirement. According to their study, France, for example, by capping immigration at 30,000 new arrivals per year and simultaneously raising the retirement age to sixty-nine, could stabilize its dependency ratio at three working-age adults per dependant, about halfway between what its dependency ratio was in 1995 (4.3) and what it would be in 2015 (2), assuming no other corrective measures were taken.

So much for the 'demographic constraint' that, as many experts and European politicians argue, makes massive immigration a vital necessity for the Old Continent. But that constraint only exists if and when alternatives are not taken into consideration. And it doesn't exist *at all* in the case of African migrants for one overriding reason: their arrival in Europe does little or nothing to improve the dependency ratio on the Old Continent. There is no doubt that African adults integrate themselves into the active population and, through their social security contributions, help finance Europe's pension systems. But counting everyone in their families, which tend on average to be larger than the European norm, those gains are offset by the cost of providing schooling, day care and health care for their children. 'Taking into account both children and parents, there is no presumption that migrants even temporarily reduce the dependency ratio', Paul Collier writes (2013: 125). The so-called 'demographic constraint' is an illusion. As we have already seen, the cost of integrating migrant workers and their families is borne by the tax payer, while the employer is allowed to pocket the economic gain of migrant labour – in other words, costs are socialized while the profit is privatized. Moreover, possible alternatives to immigration, like promoting and supporting large families, are rarely pursued with any vigour. Yet in Germany even the type of massive immigration imagined under the European Convergence scenario would not compensate for the expected dramatic population loss. In

2060, despite the arrival of 86 million third-country nationals in Europe, Germany would still have 15 million fewer inhabitants than in 2010, while France, without more immigration, would see its population increase by a mere 5 per cent. How then does one justify the a priori assumption that it would be better to integrate more immigrants into European societies than to offer Europeans incentives to have more children?[19]

European leaders have preferred to conceal the social costs of immigration rather than resort to a more effective though politically riskier solution with regard to their ageing populations: to spread the demographic dividend provided by increased longevity among everyone and not just the retirees who currently monopolize this bonus. The best way to improve the dependency ratio in an ageing Europe, and to guarantee the viability of a social safety net without equal in the world, is to make the life expectancy gains that have been accumulating over the past century more productive. And these gains are considerable. Worldwide, the average life span has jumped from thirty years two centuries ago to seventy years in 2015 – sixty-eight for men and seventy-two for women – and it should reach eighty-five by 2060. Japan and France are the world leaders, averaging seventy-nine years for men and eighty-six years for women in 2017. Remember that one could only hope to live fifty years in Europe and the United States at the beginning of the twentieth century. Now, despite a downturn recorded in 2015,[20] the life expectancy of European and American children, in the space of just a generation, is five or six years longer than that of their parents. And life spans are still expected to increase: conceivably to 120 years and beyond.[21] In this context, retirement must be reimagined from scratch. Those extra years gained can no longer be exclusively used to lengthen a life of leisurely retirement at the expense of the rest of society. Retirees themselves are often the first to find fault with decades of staying on the sidelines of society. For many of them, remaining active and useful for others has become the ultimate privilege.

Beware of 'Transfers'

I need to dispel what otherwise could become a double misunderstanding: no matter what, mass migration will lose neither its function as Africa's demographic escape valve nor its immediacy for Europe, which for obvious reasons cannot possibly ignore what is going on south of the Mediterranean. There are many African proverbs that offer variations on Horace's *nam tua res agitur, paries cum proximus ardet*, 'it becomes your concern when your neighbour's house is on fire'. So far, we have only considered the European perspective. But what can Africa hope to achieve, and what does it stand to lose, with large-scale outward migration? The question implies a response to an earlier one – who, exactly, meets whom in the migratory encounter between Africa and Europe? – that is much less obvious than it might seem, and not just because it is likely to be determined as much by chance as careful planning. On one side, there is the 'migrant', the generic term we are using to refer to everyone, from asylum seekers to refugees to economic migrants, both legal and illegal. Whatever migrants' motivations when leaving Africa, these often have nothing to do with what paths they will actually pursue, or how their lives will turn out, once they reach Europe. Will they try to blend into their host country? Keep parts of their original culture and adopt others from the new culture around them? Live exactly as they did in their countries of origin, becoming more like guest workers or cultural separatists? Or will they propagate their culture and faith, aspects of their existence that they might regard as non-negotiable? Often the migrant has no idea what he is going to do when he arrives. It is only by rubbing shoulders with their new neighbours and being forced to make a series of take-it-or-leave-it decisions that the contours of a new life will slowly take shape. In this process, the fog will be even thicker if those neighbours remain anonymous. Who exactly is supposed to welcome him? The 'residents'? This term is favoured by the European Union, but includes other immigrants from the diasporas already living in the host country. Other expressions, such as 'native French' or the evocative term *souchiens* – those who, like trees, have already put down roots in the country – are contentious. Just as contentious is the idea, not uncommon among African migrants, that they have come to live 'in the white man's home' – a notion refuted, after decades of transnational migration, by many arrivals preceding their own. To provide the Ariadne's thread out of this classificatory labyrinth, a researcher at the French Institute for Demographic Studies (INED), Michèle Tribalat, has floated the term 'native squared' – a French person whose parents and grandparents were also French. But INED, like the National Institute of Statistics and Economic Studies (INSEE), prefers instead to refer to the 'majority population' with no more precision than that, or to identify these phantom-like opposites of the newcomer with a double negative: 'neither immigrant nor descendant of an immigrant'. The awkwardness is palpable. Here not only is the reckoning done without the host, but the host cannot even be named and, as a consequence, the migrant has no identifiable counterpart. The host country is turned into an Escheresque madhouse of doors that open into thin air and stairways leading nowhere. Little wonder hosts and migrants may feel uneasy living in it together. Between them, nothing else than citizenship and the underlying social contract should matter – not skin colour, religion, ethnic origin or the status of one's parents or grandparents. The citizens of a country – all passport holders with the right to vote – are the hosts (who themselves may be former migrants or offspring of migrants). As we have already stated, they alone have the ability to decide who can join their 'club', and under what conditions, within the limits of the international obligations to which their country has freely consented.

The migratory encounter has resulted in a major transfer of money from the North to the South: 466 billion dollars in 2017 worldwide, more than three times the level of development aid. In 2017, according to World Bank figures, immigrants from sub-Saharan Africa sent back to their home countries 38

billion dollars, against 45 billion dollars of foreign direct investment and 25 billion dollars of development aid that was received
by the region that year. But these migratory remittances are
easily underestimated because they do not include the numerous
transfers of smaller sums averaging 200 dollars or so, amounts
not captured in global statistics because they are often sent
through informal channels. The difficulty in tracing these foreign
exchange flows is also due, at least in part, to striking divergences
in remittance patterns from country to country, which in turn
depend on both intra-family cultural norms but also on where
immigrants live. For example, Senegalese in Spain could hold
the world remittance record, sending back home half their earnings, while Ghanaians living in Italy share with their families
back home on average 'only' about one-quarter of their earnings
(Collier 2013: 206).

In any event, the financial support that sub-Saharan Africa
receives from its Argonauts abroad is indisputably very important.
But it is not an unalloyed benefit. First, by sending a significant
portion of their earnings to Africa, immigrants limit their ability
to fully integrate themselves and their families, including their
European-born children, into their host countries. There is
simply less money to compete with their children's peers in providing supplementary educational benefits, for private schooling
or leisure activities; less money also to spend on rent or to afford a
car. Secondly, the money sent home is rarely a productive investment. At best, it pays school fees and health-care bills, or provides
funds to build a house. But it is often used simply to make ends
meet – when it is not squandered to subsidize indolent parents or
fund the ostentatious display of wealth. In every case, however, it
deepens the social divide in villages and urban neighbourhoods
between those who have a relative living abroad and everyone
else, who are often envious and tempted to send one of their own
to Europe to even the score. Thirdly, *The Money Order* – the title
of a novel and 1968 film by the late Senegalese writer and director Ousmane Sembène – is accompanied by other 'transfers' that

are no less important, but which are rarely taken into account. Until the end of the twentieth century, there was only the annual return of the migrant for a short visit, usually in the summer, plus a few letters and postcards spread over the year and the rare telephone call on the occasion of a marriage, a funeral or the end of Ramadan. Today there is email, Facebook, Skype, Viber and WhatsApp; Wi-Fi makes more or less continual contact with the migrant's home country virtually free. This intensification of exchanges both relays and personalizes the flood of news and media images transmitted over radio and television, the internet or satellites. Family members on either side are constantly asked to decipher the latest news, to give a personal gloss on events. It is an incessant exchange of ideas, a comparative study that never ends. 'Immigration to Europe has resulted in the repatriation to the Maghreb of both sexual and familial models that have hastened the demographic transition, as opposed to what happened in Egypt, where emigration to the Gulf States has reinvigorated both conservative and natalist references', notes Jean-François Bayart. 'In sub-Saharan Africa, the exchange of views between the societies of origin and the migrant's host societies will have a similar transformative impact on kinship ties, matrimonial relations, role models, the traditional submission of youth to their elders, or women to men, but also between captives and free men' (2010: 139).

This 'backfiring', as Bayart goes on to call it, is not unidirectional. Accepted ideas in Africa that involve political or parental authority, or religious freedom or homosexuality, risk appearing 'out of bounds' in the European context as much as the normative content moving in the opposite direction in the African context. But if these European conceptions are seen to augur a future that is both sometimes desirable and sometimes detestable, the messages coming from Africa are likely to reach Europe more often than not as unwelcome echoes of the past. For example, whatever the reasons for Africa's homophobia (which include the demonization of sodomy by Western missionaries), the fact that the criminalization of relations between persons of the same sex enjoys popular support in Africa clashes with today's level of tolerance of homosexuality in Europe. In thirty-four African countries, homosexuality is punishable by law, with penalties ranging from three months to two years of confinement in Burundi, up to fourteen and fifteen years in Kenya and Ethiopia, the possibility of a life sentence in Uganda and Tanzania, and the death penalty in Mauritania, Nigeria's twelve northern states, Sudan and the southern part of Somalia under the control of the Islamist insurgency al-Shabaab.

It is not ignominious – xenophobic or racist – to oppose 'the importation of homophobia'. However, each individual migrant is not a delegate or emissary of his country or culture. In addition, whatever the mixed blessings of social transfers, they are inevitable and, whether we like it or not, exercise a relativizing effect on some of the ideas and attitudes that are held most tenaciously in both sender and receiver cultures.

'A Rancour Sharpened by the Winter'

Ironically, what is often presented as the only chance for the most destitute to escape the 'poverty trap' is also a pillage of African talent. The so-called 'brain drain' is not some minor by-product of the migratory encounter between Africa and Europe. A good third of all African-born physicians work in member countries of the OECD club of wealthiest countries. At the same time, the ratio of physicians to patients in sub-Saharan Africa is in the order of one for every 9,000 people, indeed, one for every 90,000 persons in an extreme case like that of South Sudan – a ratio between thirty and 300 times less favourable than in the UK. Overall, in the past thirty years, it is estimated that between one-third and one-half of all African university degree holders have either left their country or did not return after studying abroad, preferring to work instead in a developed country. Some researchers have claimed that brain drain is in fact a 'brain gain'. They argue that university graduates will not only send large sums of money back home, but will, by their example, encourage their compatriots to invest in the education of their children and thus initiate a virtuous circle. I have my doubts. To begin with, it is very expensive to become a university or professional school graduate in Africa (in 2005, training a medical doctor cost on average 184,000 dollars (Kohnert 2006: 3)). It would take extremely generous migrants to send that kind of money back home (and their remittances would benefit their families, not the economy at large). Secondly, the idea of wanting to turn Africa into a talent pool for Europe strikes me as an odd development strategy, all the more so because it relies on foreign volunteers – humanitarian aid workers – to come and care for the African populations left behind. To my mind, the flight of Africa's best-educated citizens, who are among the few to have the aptitude, the means and the time necessary to move their country forward, is a net loss for the continent. This abandonment is also profoundly demoralizing: the educated elite does not believe in Africa's future. They are running away.

Africa's public intellectuals, many living in Europe or America, often make critical remarks about their former colonial rulers, about Europe's rapacity yesterday and its bloodless, museum-like existence today. Whether they are right or wrong, it is easy to understand why they would see Africa's former metropoles as 'whitewashed tombs, which outwardly appear beautiful, but within are full of dead people's bones and all uncleanness' – the evangelist Matthew's simile for hypocrisy (Matt 23:27) that in turn inspired Joseph Conrad's image of Brussels as the 'sepulchral city' in *Heart of Darkness*. Achille Mbembé speaks of 'this dull ice floe that Europe is slowly becoming'. But that is generally not how Africans in Africa perceive Europe. In their eyes, Europe, twenty times richer per capita than sub-Saharan Africa, is a bright continent of abundance where everything is well-ordered and perfectly shipshape. That, too, is understandable. How would they know better? They are not there yet.

The African diaspora in Europe is often viewed as the best

guarantor of more solidarity between the two continents. There are several things that come together here, including the great distance – geographical and cultural – between the two continents that the diaspora can help bridge. Members of the diaspora in Europe can act as mediators of a sort, at once ambassadors of their home countries and dragomen – 'interpreters' – for a Europe that historically has done a bad job of reading 'ambiguous Africa', the title of George Ballandier's 1966 magnum opus, subtitled *Cultures in Collision*. But this is to assume that Europe would not ask for anything better than a proper understanding of Africa, and that these African emissaries on European soil would serve as honest brokers. It could also be that Europe is content to find intermediaries to handle an Africa suffering from postcolonial heartburn, and that the diaspora has a vested interest in maintaining this malaise. Africans installed behind 'enemy lines' would thus be able to wash away any suspicion of having concluded a separate peace with their former colonizer, and would be able to guarantee themselves a role as indispensable intermediaries between the Young Continent and the Old. Finally, from the point of view of Africans in Africa, the diaspora is their bridgehead in Europe, but it also threatens Africans *in situ* with the 'Sundiata effect': the crippled child chased from the village could return to build an empire at their expense. The example of the freed American slaves who colonized Liberia in the first half of the nineteenth century serves, in this sense, as a warning.

The contours of the African diaspora are hazy. According to the World Bank, its population is around 30 million worldwide. But the African Union, which considers its diaspora to be a sort of global Black Caucus, puts the figure as high as 168 million. In Europe, when the distinction between an African immigrant and a member of the African diaspora is made, it often implies some version of the 'grievance identity' which the African-American political scientist Shelby Steele has ascribed to American blacks who view life through the lens of victimization. In former European metropoles, postcolonial acrimony further complicates the migratory encounter, even in the long term. In France, for example, when a white *souchien* strikes up a conversation with a black compatriot, and his opening question is 'where do you come from?', he is very likely to meet with outright exasperation. 'Come on, man, are you telling me that I can't be French and black in the same breath?!' That is perfectly fair, because black and French are in no way mutually exclusive. But it is also true that in the 1920s there were less than 3,500 sub-Saharan Africans in France, only 15,000 in the 1950s, still barely more than 30,000 in the 1960s, and around 65,000 in the 1970s following a major drought in the Sahel (Gubert 2008: 45). It is also understandable, then, for the 'native squared' to think of France as a traditionally monochromatic country and to ask what appears to be a 'simple question'. But, of course, this is wrong, not only because France has changed, but because there is no such thing as a simple question in a postcolonial context. Besides, it might be just as offensive to overlook the skin colour of a compatriot. 'Are you denying my African roots? I *am* Black, can't you see that?' All too often, the postcolonial encounter is a 'lose-lose' situation.

As we have said before, the colonial past is only a particular circumstance of the migratory encounter. Outside any postcolonial context, South-North migration has its own forms of resentment. The anthropologist Arjun Appadurai, who was born in India but has made his career in the United States, wondered in his 2006 book *Fear of Small Numbers: An Essay on the Geography of Anger*:

How can so many people hate us for the very things they desperately want and seek in trying to crash our borders, get our visas, and fly, drive, sail, or swim to our shores? Why expend huge energies getting to a land you despise? . . . What happens to a person who desires, at the risk of his or her life, what he or she so utterly despises – a 'wrong', morally flawed lifestyle? What happens when the demography of desired objects no longer forms a landscape of beauty and happiness? So, sadly, the dreamers and the haters are not two groups. They are often one and the same persons. In our globalizing world, all want to be part of the 'better world' but the better world cannot be properly defined: it's the West, for the body, and the Rest for the soul. (2006: 121, 124)

The Senegalese poet and his country's first president, Léopold Sédar Senghor, makes a similar point in a line from one of his first poems, 'Le Portrait', when he writes of 'the obstinacy of my rancour sharpened by the winter'.

Europe's 'politics of pity', to use Hannah Arendt's phrase again, prevents the continent of opulence from understanding the resentment that it arouses and the deep disappointment that it can cause. Since African migrants are escaping from 'hell', Europe must be a paradise, and once the migrants arrive, they are 'saved' – no need to worry about them anymore. The Old World should know better from its own experience: one-third of Europe's migrants, among the millions who left for the United States at the turn of the twentieth century, returned from America and its dream of a better life.[22] Today, there are not many African migrants who decide to return definitively to their home countries. 'We've come too far *not* to succeed', many of them say.[23] They cling to the hope that, at least for their children, their uprooting will lead to an irreversible gain. But in many conversations with members of the diaspora, including some of its most successful, there are often long moments of silence before a short phrase is uttered in a lowered voice: 'It's true I earn a good living here', they concede. 'But am I really living?' Then a long pause again, followed by a burst of newfound conviction. 'Well, it's done', they conclude. But their offspring, if they have grown up without a clear answer from their parents, might wonder whether it was the right thing to do.

By Way of Conclusion:
Some Plausible Scenarios for the Future

The massive migration of Africans to Europe is in the interest of neither Young Africa nor the Old Continent. For Europe, only the very selective entry of a limited number of Africans will provide any benefit because of its highly competitive and vertical job market, which is likely to contract further as automation and especially robotics continue apace: in the end, the decline in its working population will almost certainly be a net gain for Europe, not a loss. Africa, on the other hand, has far more to lose than to win from the large-scale 'exportation' of its youth. They are its hope for a better future and will be the key to its success as soon as conditions on the continent allow them to 'grow up', when there is enough remunerative work for them to become productive and independent. From this perspective, Africa's challenge is not an excess of young people but a lack of adults. However, if all these good reasons could prevent the rush towards Europe, Africa's rural exodus would never have occurred in the first place. Indeed, in the absence of both a green and an industrial revolution, the massive departure of villagers towards cities that have not been transformed into production sites also results in a lose-lose situation.[1] Yet this has not impeded the rural exodus, nor will it forestall the rush towards Europe. For both, the logic is implacable. The 'leavers' don't make their decisions based solely on an economic calculus. Whether they are villagers or inter-continental migrants, they turn their backs on what they know only too well – shortcomings, really – and take a leap of faith for the unknown. Not for one moment do they imagine that their long-time dream might be unrecognizable when it becomes their newfound reality. Africa's outward migration will be as unstoppable as has been its rural exodus. Even if a fellow countryman or 'brother' from the diaspora were to swallow his pride and concede that there are certain failures at the end of the road, the departing African would not take his word for it – no more than Africa's villagers have listened to their 'brothers' who have moved to the continent's cities that are mostly slums. Everybody *wants* a better future and wants to see it with their own eyes. Even when it seems elusive, isn't it better to keep looking for it than to give up?

Africa, a continent that is still poor but already a demographic billionaire – and will become a demographic multi-billionaire within thirty years – is knocking on Europe's door. Not only is its population growing, but it is by far the youngest in the world. Between the Tropics of Cancer and Capricorn, four Africans out of ten are less than fifteen years old, and seven out of ten are under thirty. The balance between the past and the future is heavily tilted towards the future. A growing number of these young Africans have the means and the informed view of the world that allow them to leave in search of a better life wherever the prospects are bright. And that better life is not just a reverie: they see it on satellite TV and the internet; they are partaking in modernity by 'screen-shopping' around the clock. Some of their brothers and sisters are already living in the Global North, where this virtual reality is reality *tout court*. So the most audacious or enterprising – sometimes the least stable as well – will head out to Europe, the closest emporium (and sometimes their former imperial metropole). The scale of the migratory encounter between

Young Africa and the Old Continent is about to change, but there is still room and time for Africans and Europeans to make choices, ideally in concert with one another. They can organize what they can't prevent. They can finally confront a challenge that will become hugely problematic for both of them unless they seize the opportunity to 'refound' their neighbourly relationship. It is getting late, however, and the past throws a disturbing shadow over the future. Decades of inaction, of irresponsibility and partisan entrenchment do not bode well for the kind of demographic governance that is urgently needed. In Europe, the myth of economic necessity that surrounds labour migration – a technocratic *fait accompli* rather than a democratic choice – fosters the temptation to 'let it run its course', likewise the myth in Africa that persistently high fertility rates are a form of wealth, rather than a guarantee of poverty for all. Both illusions increase the likelihood that African migratory flows towards Europe will become a scramble. When? As soon as Africa, above all sub-Saharan Africa, really emerges from its underdevelopment. This is the quandary that Europeans will have to live with for the next two generations: good news out of Africa will be bad news for them.

The Obsession with 'Scenes and Types'

I would like to conclude with a few plausible scenarios for the future. The first, the 'Eurafrica' scenario, presupposes a reservoir of goodwill towards African immigrants, who are viewed as the best chance of investing the Old Continent with a younger, more diverse, and possibly more dynamic population. This would seal the 'Americanization' of Europe in the unstinting language of the poet Emma Lazarus engraved on the base of the Statue of Liberty: 'Give me your tired, your poor / Your huddled masses yearning to breathe free / The wretched refuse of your teeming shore. / Send these, the homeless, the tempest-tost to me / I lift my lamp beside the golden door!' Like America, Europe would fully embrace migration and become a genuine melting pot.[2] This scenario would also consecrate the triumph of a humanistic universalism. Germany, in the summer of 2015, comes to mind (even though 80 per cent of the migrants then came from Syria and other war-torn countries in the Middle East and Asia, and not from Africa). In welcoming a million migrants, ready to share their country with them, many Germans experienced the collective enchantment of living in perfect accord with their moral principles, an epiphany of their 'ethics of conviction'.[3] The father of the concept, Max Weber, compared this intimate consonance with that of a Christian fulfilling his duty, adding: 'As for the outcome of his action, the believer simply trusts in God.' Which is also what humanitarian aid workers are doing in the Mediterranean. They retrieve migrants whose only desire is to 'live decently', even if that means putting their lives – and the lives of their children – in danger and blackmailing Europe. NGOs fulfil the duty to rescue depositing migrants safely on Europe's coasts. But how do these NGOs respond to the editorialist who accuses them of raising money to 'save' these migrants but then stopping their charity mid-stream, 'without finding work, lodging or schooling for the poor souls whom they have helped to reach Europe?'[4]

The 'ethics of responsibility' – according to Weber 'the political attitude par excellence' – obliges us to take responsibility for our acts beyond a moral narcissism, in all of their foreseeable consequences. And 'Eurafrica' would mean the end of social security in Europe as we know it, because a welfare state without borders is unsustainable – the contract of intergenerational solidarity on which it rests can only apply within a demarcated area. It is one thing to invite foreigners into a society to share its riches; but it is an entirely different thing to share with them the *capacity* of a society *to create* those riches – if that were easy, development aid would not be the failure it is, and African migrants would not be fleeing their countries in the first place. A developed state with a reliable social safety net cannot practise an open-door policy, hence the historical absence of social security worthy of the name in immigrant nations such as the United States. If Europe were to follow the American example, the Old World would inevitably come to resemble the New World: its 'social state' would wither away and leave behind only Hobbes's Leviathan, busy preventing 'the war of all against all'. That would be a tall order in societies that are used to a high level not only of social security but of shared cultural codes – Putnam's 'bonding capital' – and the command of the repertoire demanded by those codes. 'Eurafrica' might even end up regretting the border controls, visible barriers and document checks inasmuch as the nagging question of 'who is my neighbour?' is increasingly internalized in a rapidly globalizing world. At each contact with the 'other', our internal sentinels cry: 'Who goes there?' This incessant work of patrolling difference compels everyone to exhibit their identity the best they can and heightens the importance of physical markers for the simple reason of expediency: bodily features such as skin colour, tattoos and biometrics display identity just as clearly as tribal scarifications.

Liberal democracy – a political system founded on the right to hold different opinions, and the assumption of shifting majorities – is emptied of its deliberative sense by these all too 'natural' marks of conviction and belonging inscribed on the body. So-called 'identity politics' in the United States affords us a glimpse of the future. It shares with colonialism – a massive and unequal encounter with otherness – an obsession with 'scenes and types'.

The second scenario, 'Fortress Europe', is already familiar, and even notorious in the eyes of many for being a losing battle fought for a shameful cause. Yet, if one stops to consider the facts, there is a case to be made for it, and perhaps it has a reasonable chance of success. To begin with, securing Europe's border would help to narrow the gap – an abyss, really – between the right of asylum and the moral principles underlying it, on the one hand, and the realities of South-North migration on the other. 'Between the early 1970s and the late 1990s the number of asylum applications in the countries that now comprise the European Union increased twenty-fold – from about 15,000 per annum to more than 300,000' (Hatton 2004: 7).[5] Since 2000, this three-decade-long upward trend has continued unabated: in 2014, the year before the 'migration crisis', the number of first-time asylum seekers in the EU was 562,700; in 2017, after the migratory peak, Eurostat put it at 650,000. What accounts for such a stupendous rise in asylum requests? Has the world really become so much more dangerous over the past half century, in particular in the new democracies south of the Sahara like Senegal, the Ivory Coast, Ghana, Nigeria or Kenya? In 2017, according to Eurostat, four out of five asylum seekers in Europe – 82 per cent – were under the age of thirty-five and two-thirds of them – 68 per cent – were men. This is not the demography of the lifeboats . . . Also in 2017, 54 per cent of first-instance asylum decisions in the twenty-eight EU countries resulted in rejections – a figure that masks huge disparities, from Ireland (11 per cent) to the Czech Republic (88 per cent) by way of Germany (50 per cent), the UK (69 per cent) and France (71 per cent). In 2016, when the number of claimants was twice as high, Germany had rejected 91 per cent of initial applications, and Portugal, Croatia, Estonia and Lithuania a staggering 100 per cent. This means, for one thing, that the right of asylum in the EU has become a game of chance depending on the member state where the request is made and on the overall number of claimants from one year to the next. But it also suggests that right of asylum has become a fig leaf for economic migration. As advocates of a 'Fortress Europe' approach could convincingly argue, only by rigorously securing its borders will the EU create the condition of the possibility of also defending the right of asylum – whether Europe would actually do so, and how exactly, remain nonetheless open questions. But, currently, right of asylum is denied in courtrooms across the continent to hundreds of thousands of migrants of whom only a small fraction are deported – their repatriation is a major logistical and financial challenge, and even an impossibility when their home countries refuse to readmit them. As a result, popular resentment against immigration is fuelled by anxieties that the rules are being taken advantage of. It is not so much that it is hard to understand why migrants would want to enter Europe without any legitimate grounds for doing so. More to the point: what guarantee do Europeans have that, after submitting an unsuccessful membership application, but staying on in any case, these newcomers will play by their rules?

On a practical level, 'Fortress Europe' is not as indefensible as it might at first seem. Public opinion and the political leaders keen to follow it will almost always backtrack when their generosity is at odds with their own interests. Germany again comes to mind, but also Italy, which has been on the front line of the immigration influx. Even before the advent of an anti-migrant 'government of change' in May 2018 – a coalition built around a populist movement and an extreme-right party – Rome had limited the actions of NGOs operating in the Mediterranean, equipped the Libyan coast guard (such as it is), sent in the Italian navy, and engaged in unspecified 'exchanges' with Libyan warlords in the absence of a legitimate government able to enforce its decisions on the ground.[6] The result was dramatic. Suddenly, in the summer of 2017, the flow of migrants from Libya dropped as abruptly as the 6 billion euros granted to Turkey have restricted inflows into Europe's southeast flank. If one adds to this the subterfuge and behind-the-scenes operations of the various European secret services, the Old Continent seems less toothless than its senile caricature. With the tacit or perhaps faint-hearted consent of public opinion, simply happy just to see the former flood of immigrants drop to a trickle – no matter the actual reasons underlying the change – Europe has the means to tighten its borders. After all, the continent is rich, and those clambering to get in come for the most part from poor countries that can be paid off. However, any attempt to stem Africa's 'scramble for Europe' through security measures alone is destined to fail.

Go See the Other Side!

A third scenario would be a 'Mafia Drift'. The naivety with which human traffickers are still perceived in many quarters as 'Robin Hoods with a penchant for lucre' obfuscates this very real danger. In the 1990s, debating 'greed vs grievances', conflict analysis rediscovered the Machiavellian insight that insurgencies occur simply when they are 'doable' – that is to say, when an unscrupulous political or military entrepreneur is capable of making one happen, and not merely when legitimate claims remain unaddressed and people take up arms as a last resort. By the same token, more research on migration is likely to show that the entrenchment of international networks of human traffickers is not simply an enabling condition but a cause of migration. Like war, migration is both frightening and exhilarating – an adventure – and the smugglers are lords and masters of the game. Then too, a 'Mafia Drift' is favoured by the likelihood of human smugglers joining forces or starting a war with organized crime in Europe, as already happens in drug trafficking, and as was true in the late 1990s when smuggling operations from Albania to southern Italy peaked, with the connivance of the Italian mafias.

The extent to which human trafficking already resembles a latter-day slave trade is revealed in an excellent piece of reportage which appeared in April 2017 in *The New Yorker*. Its author, Ben Taub, writes:

> More than eleven thousand Nigerian women were rescued in the Mediterranean last year, according to the International Organization for Migration, eighty per cent of whom had been trafficked for sexual exploitation. 'You now have girls who are thirteen, fourteen, fifteen,' an IOM anti-trafficking agent told me. 'The market is requesting younger and younger.' Italy is merely the entry point; from there, women are traded and sold to madams all over Europe.

Sex trafficking provides only a glimpse of a broader criminal division of labour that could ultimately backfire against smugglers, traffickers and migrants, especially if the European underworld ever finds a far-right political patron. Just as we saw during the decolonization of North Africa in the late 1950s, we could then witness the rise of terrorist organizations like La Main Rouge (The Red Hand) – an informal operation run by French counter-intelligence – which carried out acts of sabotage and targeted assassinations in the name of keeping Algeria French. With or without the collusion of intelligence services, extremist supporters of Europe's 'defence' would almost certainly bolster their ranks.

Nor should we exclude the possibility of another scenario, however remote it might seem to us now: 'The Return of the Protectorate'. In the face of an unprecedented migratory influx that could be framed as an existential threat to its 'civilization', Europe could revert to its old reflexes and 'cut out the evil at its source'. This pre-emptive defence could mobilize two time-tested techniques of colonial governance: the politics of 'divide and rule' and elite co-optation. Europe could form pacts with various African governments ready to stop their own citizens from leaving on the basis of quid-pro-quo arrangements. This is already the case on the other side of the Mediterranean, from Morocco to Libya, and in the Sahel region. Such arrangements often appear under anodyne headings such as: 'Co-management of migratory flows'. In exchange for development aid with no strings attached, and for visas granting freedom of movement throughout Europe to members of local elites – not only politicians but also business people, academics and artists – 'co-operative' countries could become de facto 'protectorates' of Europe in both senses of the word: their regimes would be sheltered from bothersome outside interference at the same time as their sovereignty would be infringed for the sake of Europe's tranquillity. Beyond this, it is anybody's guess whether public disenchantment, which has been growing in Africa since independence, could be mobilized to instigate and justify even more overt neo-colonial takeovers.

A final scenario – 'Bric-a-brac Politics' – may seem underwhelming by absolute standards, but is highly compatible with the erratic functioning of modern democracies, which are driven by electoral cycles, ever shorter news cycles and constant opinion polling. This scenario involves a modest dose of all the previous options in combination. Spain is a good example. A traditional and longstanding land of emigration that experienced a baby-boom in the 1960s and 1970s before its fertility rate plunged, Spain had few immigrants until the end of the twentieth century: in 1990, they accounted for 0.9 per cent of its population. Twenty years later, 14 per cent of its population, according to Eurostat – 12 per cent, according to the Spanish government – were born outside the country, a number that included some 800,000 Moroccans. Yet in a country where historically *no hay moros en la costa* ('there are no Moors on the coast') is the proverbial negation of imminent danger, no anti-migrant groundswell has benefited a far-right extremist party or populist movement. Spain has absorbed migratory flows and shirked the consequences; sometimes it has dodged them altogether. It negotiated in 2000 a Global Programme of Regulation and Coordination of Foreign Residents' Affairs and Immigration – the 'Greco Plan' – and has taken a pragmatic approach to improving its cooperation with Morocco, Mauritania and Senegal. These measures, no doubt helped by a harsh economic crisis, have made a difference. In 2015, and with very little attention paid by the media, the European country that is geographically closest to Africa received only 13,000 asylum demands out of a total of 1.25 million for all of Europe. In 2016, the percentage of foreigners living in Spain dropped below 10 per cent. Of course, it could go up again, and there are signs that it will, now that the central migratory route across the Mediterranean – from Libya to Italy – has become much more difficult for migrants. But in essence, a 'flexible' management of migratory flows is making a wager on a future of *real* prosperity in Africa, similar to that which now entices Mexicans living in the United States to set off again for their homeland. After all, it only has to hold off, one way or the other, for another two or three generations. Will that be possible if a 'scramble for Europe' takes place? I don't think so, but 'muddling through' will be part of Europe's future – not the most courageous and resolute part of it, but certainly not the least humane, and perhaps not the least astute.

Many years ago, when I arrived in Berlin to undertake studies at its 'Free University', I realized I had fallen into a trap that two generations of Germans – my friends and their parents – had set up for each other. Any complaints about the political system, or potential efforts to change it, were met with the same peremptory response: 'If you don't like it here, then go and live on the other side', they would say, meaning the other side of the Berlin Wall and the demonstrably poorer city of East Berlin, the capital of the German Democratic Republic, a Warsaw Pact member firmly in the Soviet camp. In addition to the wall dividing Berlin into two parts, the GDR also needed a *Todesstreifen* – a heavily fortified minefield that ran the length of the whole country and was guarded by soldiers in watchtowers ready to shoot anyone who attempted to cross into the West.

For Africans today, it is the opposite. They are surrounded by obstacles – from high fences in Ceuta and Melilla, through a *limes* of police states all around the Mediterranean and across the Sahel, to an invisible wall of money – that Europeans have erected to prevent them from leaving their continent by crossing the *Mare nostrum*. Often the older ones encourage the younger ones to try their hand at this adventure. '*Go and live on the other side!*', is more or less what they say. And young Africans go, no matter the cost, though they only have the vaguest idea of what awaits them beyond the barriers. But they feel imprisoned and confined, and they flee their continent in order to free themselves. I can understand them, yet believe they are wrong – headed in the wrong direction, if not for their individual future, then for the destiny of

their continent. As I wrote this book I often found myself won-
dering how different Africa would be if all that energy expended
to leave the continent were turned inward. What would that look
like?

Notes

Introduction

1 'Britain's Most Racist Election: The Story of Smethwick, 50 Years On', *Guardian*, 15 October 2014; 'On the Brink of Brexit, Voters Reflect: "I Feel More Strongly Now, Let's Get Out"', *Guardian*, 18 March 2017; 'Smethwick: What Happened to the English Town that Once Tried to Ban Non-Whites from Buying Homes?', *International Business Times*, 20 December 2013. In 1951, 2.8 per cent of Smethwick's inhabitants were born outside of the UK; in 2011, 13.5 per cent of its households didn't count a single person using English as their 'main language of communication'.

2 The 1951 Refugee Convention was originally an instrument of the Cold War aimed at protecting dissidents fleeing Eastern Europe's communist countries. A 1967 Protocol removed its temporal and geographic restrictions and conferred on the UN High Commissioner for Refugees (UNHCR) a universal mandate. Many millions of asylum seekers are interim beneficiaries of the Convention, as a result of signatory states' interpretations, such as 'leave to remain' in the UK. But only 2 per cent – roughly half a million people – of the world's refugees today (roughly 25 million) have acceded to one of the three permanent solutions which

the Convention proposes: return to their home country once it has become safe again; integration in their country of refuge; or settlement in a third country prepared to welcome them permanently. The Convention does not consider 'economic' hardship as persecution: it does not constitute grounds for asylum. In practice, the distinction between economic refugees and asylum seekers is enforced by host countries according to the prevailing mood of their governments, their press and their law courts. Germany took in almost 1 million asylum seekers in 2015, but the following year rejected 91 per cent of the requests for protection that had been introduced. After a rejection, a lengthy appeal process is likely to ensue, in which a number of the original rejections are overturned, while others go on into the thickets of the legal system.

3 Over the same period, the number of South-South migrants increased from 60 to 80 million.

4 See also Ross Douthat, 'The Scramble for Europe', *New York Times*, 8 August 2015. According to UN projections, the arrival of 80 million migrants in EU countries over fifty years would result in a first or second-generation immigrant population of 26 per cent (United Nations Population Division 2000: 90).

5 For Africa as a whole, 41 per cent of the population is under fifteen. But there are significant disparities. North Africa (31 per cent) has almost completed its demographic transition while the population pyramid of southern Africa (30 per cent) is heavily impacted by the AIDS epidemic. Central Africa (46 per cent) and West Africa (43 per cent) – roughly forty states – are the most youthful parts of the continent. They lie at the core of my argument.

6 According to Marc Sommers (2015: 321), the term was coined by a political scientist, Gary Fuller, in a study commissioned by the CIA. Other authors cite Gunnar Heinsohn, a sociologist who taught at the University of Bremen (Germany), as the father of the concept in the mid-1990s. Technically, a population pyramid evinces a 'youth bulge' when the cohort aged between fifteen and twenty-nine accounts for 40 per cent or more of the total adult population, defined as those between eighteen and sixty-four.

7 I owe this figure to my friend and colleague in Cultural Anthropology

at Duke, Charles Piot, whose book on the 'diversity lottery' – based on fieldwork in Togo and the United States – is forthcoming.

8 Pew Research Center, 24 March 2017: www.pewresearch.org/fact-tank/2017/03/24/applications-for-u-s-visa-lottery-more-than-doubled-since-2007.

9 'Les migrations africaines vers l'Europe ont toutes les raisons de croître', *L'Opinion*, 15 December 2016. According to polls run by Gallup between 2013 and 2016, overall 31 per cent of sub-Saharan Africans intend to migrate, against a worldwide average of 14 per cent.

10 Pew Research Center, 22 March 2018: www.pewglobal.org/2018/03/22/at-least-a-million-sub-saharan-africans-moved-to-eu rope-since-2010.

11 'Migrations africaines, le défi de demain', *Le Monde*, 16 January 2017.

12 'Migrants: l'échec moral de l'Union européenne', *Le Monde*, 8 September 2017.

13 This position suffered a sharp rebuke in the September 2017 federal elections, which saw German Chancellor Angela Merkel's CDU/CSU party receive its lowest share of the vote since 1949, and the nativist Alternative for Germany win representation in the Bundestag for the first time; indeed, Merkel has since refrained from repeating her previous call that there should be no *Obergrenze* or 'cap' on immigration.

14 Among them, most notably, Jean-Claude Chesnais, Jean-Claude Chasteland and Herwig Birg.

15 I use SAIS – where I taught from 2007 to 2013 – as an example because its Africa programme, with a ringside seat for policy making in Washington DC, is more than many other African studies departments resolutely turned towards engaging with the continent's realities.

16 The subtitle of the English version, released in 2018 by Oxford University Press, is 'Development or Jihad'.

17 See http://blogs.worldbank.org/africacan/africa-s-statistical-tragedy.

18 See Melber (2016) and the monthly publication by the NGO Africa Good Governance, *Africa in Fact*, November 2014, 'Making up the Middle'.

1 The Law of Large Numbers

1 According to Rita Headrick (1994), basic public health services were up and running in all colonies that were part of French Equatorial Africa (AEF) by 1910. Chasteland and Chesnais insist on the synergy between better public health care and infrastructural improvements: 'During the interwar period, a worldwide sanitary revolution was underway; the later it occurred, the more important was the demographic surge it triggered: the benefits of medical discoveries and socio-economic innovations combined their effects. From then on, in countries where the fertility rate had not yet dropped, annual demographic growth rates could reach 3 per cent, and even 4 per cent' (2006: 1003). This was the case, in particular, in sub-Saharan Africa.

2 In the references, 'loc.' refers to the location in the Kindle edition of the work cited.

3 Chasteland and Chesnais highlight the nexus between the Industrial Revolution, demographic transition and emigration in Great Britain: 'Between 1750 and 1900, demographic growth in the United Kingdom resulted in a six-fold increase of the number of its inhabitants, and the swarming-out of its surplus population across the world (with the exception of continental Europe). In particular, this movement gave birth to the United States' (2006: 1003–4).

4 The population density in Europe (without Russia) is roughly a hundred inhabitants per square kilometre, an average that, as in Africa, masks great disparities. These range from Spain (86) to the United Kingdom (247), to France (112) and Germany (231). The average population density in Asia is eighty-seven inhabitants per square kilometre, and that of China and India, respectively, 150 and 390 inhabitants per square kilometre.

5 Null bases his study on the median scenario of the UN projections for the end of the century, i.e. 3.36 billion people in sub-Saharan Africa in 2100.

6 Projects such as Eko Atlantic can be found across the African continent, from the New Cairo in Egypt to Waterfall City in South Africa, between Johannesburg and Pretoria, to Hope City, a 10-billion-dollar project in Ghana, Kakungulu Satellite City on the outskirts of Kampala, in Uganda, Malili Ranch near Nairobi, which

is vaunted by its promoters as 'Kenya's Silicon Valley' and, finally, Kilamba City, Luanda's satellite city that was built by Chinese companies in Angola and has become the most expensive city in the world. This spatial compartmentalization – segregation would be another word – puts one in mind of the 'colonial city' as described by Frantz Fanon in *The Wretched of the Earth*. If you replace in the following passage his 'settlers' and 'colonized' by 'the rich' and 'the poor', it reads: 'The sector inhabited by the poor is not complementary to the sector inhabited by the rich. The two confront each other, but not in the service of a higher unity. Governed by a purely Aristotelian logic, they follow the dictates of mutual exclusion: There is no conciliation possible, one of them is superfluous. . . . The gaze that the poor casts at the part of town where the rich live is a look of lust, a look of envy. Dreams of possession. Every type of possession: of sitting at the rich man's table and sleeping in his bed, preferably with his wife' (2004: 4, 5).

7   BBC News, 11 September 2015, www.bbc.com/news/world-africa-34188248.

8   Sheng Yun, 'Little Emperors', *London Review of Books*, 19 May 2016; Simon Leplâtre, 'En Chine, pas de réveil démographique', *Le Monde*, 4 January 2017; Isabelle Attané, 'En Chine, l'enfant unique . . . le restera', *Le Monde*, 26 November 2013.

9   In her 2003 dissertation, discussing 'The Global, the Local, and Population Policy in Sub-Saharan Africa', Rachel Sullivan notes: 'Unlike the standard diffusion story, in which the most modern actors play the role of innovators, I find that the first countries to adopt policies actually had lower levels of governmental capacity and were more traditional than those who adopted policies later or that did not adopt policies at all. I explain this paradox based on these countries' greater desire to signal their modernity to outsiders, and their relatively weak position vis-à-vis powerful external organizations like the World Bank.'

10 'Afrique, le grand rattrapage démographique', Interview in *Le Monde*, 15 December 2007.

11 Quoted in 'Africa. Who is Safe?', *Time* Magazine, 13 March 1964.

2 The Island-Continent of Peter Pan

1 *Machete Season: The Killers in Rwanda Speak* is a book by Jean Hatzfeld, published in 2003 in French and in 2006 in English. In it, the author reports testimonies of convicted perpetrators of the Rwandan genocide.

2 While there are important differences between Zimbabwe and South Africa, the 'land question' also looms large over the former land of apartheid. A quarter century after the end of racial discrimination, 87 per cent of the privately owned land in South Africa belongs to whites, who represent roughly 10 per cent of the population; between 50,000 and 60,000 modern farms managed by whites put under the plough 72 per cent of the available cropland; the post-apartheid objective of purchasing and transferring 30 per cent of this farmland to black owners by 2015 has been missed, and by a margin: only 3 per cent has changed hands. At the current pace, meeting the target will take a century, and this provided the government allocates to land reform more than the 0.4 per cent of its budget it has dedicated to redressing the land imbalance since the end of apartheid.

3 Lydia Polgreen, 'In Zimbabwe Land Takeover, a Golden Lining', *New York Times*, 20 July 2012; Tony Hawkins, 'Counting the Cost of Zimbabwean Land Reform', *politicsweb*, 1 November 2012, www.politicsweb.co.za/news-and-analysis/counting-the-cost-of-zimbabwean-land-reform.

4 For a recent critical assessment of Museveni's regime, with heavy emphasis on US involvement, see Epstein 2017.

5 Riffing on the born-again leitmotiv 'Jesus is the answer', Ruth Marshall (2009) asked 'But if Jesus is the answer, what is the question?'; for my remarks on charismatic churches in Africa, I draw on her book, in particular chapter 2 ('Rupture, Redemption, and the History of the Present') and chapter 5 ('Born-Again Ethics and the Spirits of the Political Economy').

6 In the latest English edition of Isabelle Eberhardt's book, translated by Sharon Banger and released by Peter Owen Publishers in 2004, the title – *In the Shadow of Islam* – oddly omits the homage paid by its author to her adopted religion. The French original, *Dans l'ombre chaude de l'Islam*, was first published in 1906, two years after

Eberhardt, at age twenty-seven, had perished in a flash flood in the Algerian desert.

7 The date chosen for the inaugural attacks of the ANC's armed wing Umkhonto we Sizwe, 'The Spear of the Nation', was chiefly motivated by the commemoration of the Battle of Blood River, which – in Afrikaner mythology – had resulted in the victory of 470 of their *Voortrekkers*, or 'pioneers', over more than 10,000 Zulu warriors on the bank of the Ncome River on 16 December 1838.

8 Interview with Catherine Nay on the private radio station Europe 1, 4 February 1990.

3 Emerging Africa

1 In the context of the Cold War, Walt Rostow's *The Stages of Economic Development: A Non-Communist Manifesto*, published in 1960, was highly influential in reasserting orthogenesis and holding up the European path of development as a 'model' for the rest of the world. It argued that all nations followed the same pattern of 'modernization' transitioning through five stages: traditional society, preconditions for take-off, take-off, drive to maturity, and high mass consumption.

2 Edward Said's book *Orientalism* was published in 1978; ten years later, Valentin Mudimbé (1988) applied his analytical grit to Africa, under the title *The Invention of Africa: Gnosis, Philosophy, and the Order of Knowledge*.

3 *The Bright Continent* is the title of Dayo Olopade's excellent book (2014), which seeks to wrong-foot the reader's gloomy expectations. While it highlights positive change in modern Africa, it is not 'Afrocentrist'.

4 Cf. *Africa in Fact*, November 2014, 'Making up the Middle'.

5 Part of Uwem Akpan's award-winning collection *Say You're One of Them* (2008).

6 T. S. Eliot, 'Whispers of Immortality', 1919.

7 In *The Village of Waiting*, Packer (1984) recounts his year-long experience as a Peace Corps instructor in the Togolese village Lavié – the name means 'wait a little more'.

4 A Cascade of Departures

1 See www.wider.unu.edu/publication/global-distribution-household-wealth.

2 See https://inequality.org/facts/global-inequality.

3 Co-development is a concept that was forged in 1997 by a French scholar, Samir Naïr, and considers migrants to be a developing factor for their country of origin as well as a net gain for their host country. In addition to the development aid provided by the host country, the remittances that are sent home by migrants are supposed to develop their country of origin and, in the long term, extinguish the incentive to migrate.

4 The data on Niger that follow are drawn from Michaïlof's book.

5 Quoted by Laurence Caramel, 'Un milliard de citadins dans vingt ans: l'Afrique est-elle prête?', Le Monde, 30 July 2017.

6 To provide just one example for the migratory diversity: the Bwas in southeastern Mali migrate on a large scale – in 2010, three out of four male youngsters under the age of twenty, and almost all girls, had spent a period of their life outside their ethnic homeland – but hardly ever beyond Mali itself or a neighbouring country. The main purpose of their migration is the acquisition of Bambara, Mali's most widely spoken language, and they do not move beyond the region where this idiom is used. For more detail see Hertrich and Lesclingand (2013).

7 See Jérôme Tubiana, 'Short Cuts', London Review of Books, 15 June 2018.

8 See https://data.worldbank.org/indicator/SH.STA.MMRT. In 2015, for all of sub-Saharan Africa, the risk for a woman of dying in childbirth was 0.99 per cent. Of course, the statistical likelihood of death is totally irrelevant for anyone who loses a loved one. No one mourning the loss of a relative or a friend in a plane crash would find any consolation in the fact that, statistically speaking, one could take a flight every day for 123,000 years before dying in an accident. In the same way, the risk calculations for crossing the Mediterranean as a migrant offer no consolation for the death of Alan Kurdi or any of the others who have perished on their way to Europe.

9 Stuart A. Thompson and Anjali Singhvi, 'Efforts to Rescue Migrants

Caused Deadly, Unexpected Consequences', *New York Times*, 14 June 2017, www.nytimes.com/interactive/2017/06/14/world/eur ope/migrant-rescue-efforts-deadly.html.

10 Jason Horowitz, 'For Right-Wing Italian Youth, a Mission to Disrupt Migration', *New York Times*, 21 July 2017, www.nytimes. com/2017/07/21/world/europe/for-right-wing-italian-youth-a-mis sion-to-disrupt-migration.html.

5 *Europe as Destination and Destiny*

1 According to a UN study already cited (UN Population Division 2000: 90), it would take 79.4 million immigrants in forty-five years to maintain the same workforce Europe had in 1995. Under this scenario, 25.7 per cent of Europe's population would be first or second-generation immigrants in 2050.

2 See www.nytimes.com/2018/05/28/world/europe/paris-migrant-he ro-spiderman.html.

3 See www.lemonde.fr/idees/article/2016/01/31/cologne-lieu-de-fan tasmes_4856694_3232.html.

4 According to a *Washington Post* article from 27 February 2016, some of the loudest voices at anti-immigrant rallies across Germany belong to recent immigrants and former refugees. See Rick Noack, 'Why so Many Immigrants in Germany are Opposed to the Refugee Influx', www.washingtonpost.com/news/worldviews/wp/ 2016/02/27/why-many-migrants-in-germany-are-opposed-to-the-refugee-influx/?utm_term=.59184247fa2f.

5 'Migrants Besiege Gateway to Europe', *International New York Times*, 28 February 2014.

6 *Le Monde*, 15 September 2017. Also in *Le Monde*, on 23 September 2017, Vincent Cochetel, UNHCR's Special Envoy for the Central Mediterranean Situation, declared that 'European governments must stop deluding themselves that they can work with this country. Our role, as a UN agency, is unfortunately very limited. Even if we are present in the official prisons, where between 7,000 and 9,000 migrants and asylum seekers are held, out of 390,000 in total. Others suffer inhumane treatment in detention centres run by traffickers. In the "official" prisons, we currently only have permission to speak to people from seven nationalities: Iraqis, Palestinians,

Somalis, Syrians, Ethiopians if they are Oromos, Sudanese from Darfur, and Eritreans. That means we have not yet spoken to a South Sudanese, a Malian, a Yemenite, etc.'

7   According to Reece Jones, author of *Violent Borders: Refugees and the Right to Move* (2016), only fifteen countries had built walls or wire-mesh fences on their borders in 1990; by 2016 that number had jumped to seventy.

8   I borrow from Taylor many of my immigration statistics; see also Ted Widmer, 'The Immigration Dividend', *International New York Times*, 7 October 2015; and David Brooks, 'A Little Reality on Immigration', *International New York Times*, 20 and 21 February 2016.

9   Pew Research Center, 'African Immigrant Population to the U.S. Steadily Climbs', 14 February 2017, www.pewresearch.org/fact-tank/2017/02/14/african-immigrant-population-in-u-s-steadily-climbs.

10 See 'Influx of African Immigrants Shifting National and New York Demographics', *New York Times*, 1 September 2014, which reported that 10 per cent of the inhabitants of the Bronx were Africans, and that the number of African immigrants to the whole country had grown 39 per cent between 2000 and 2011, adding: 'During that single decade, according to the most reliable estimates, more black Africans arrived in this country on their own than were imported directly to North America during the more than three centuries of the slave trade', or around 400,000 Africans.

11 See www.migrationpolicy.org/article/sub-saharan-african-immigra nts-united-states.

12 Putnam (2000) and http://bowlingalone.com; see also Sander and Putnam (2010).

13 In a co-written article published in 2010, Putnam partly revised his initial analysis. He noted that the post-9/11 generation had socially 're-engaged', inter alia to mobilize support for Barack Obama's election. But Putnam continued to advocate a strong push towards social capital. Cf. Sander and Putnam (2010).

14 Japan's 'policy of isolation' – *sakoku* – was not a pure rejection of the outside world. It was also a response to powerful domestic imperatives, in particular the desires of the *shoguns* of the Tokugawa

Clan to cut off their vassals – the *daimyos* – from the source of their wealth. By the same token, culturalist explanations, based on a 'xenophobic tradition' or the highly formalized distinction between interior and exterior – *uchi* and *soto* – are insufficient.

15 'In Japan, No Angry Populism', *International New York Times*, 9 February 2017.

16 'Focus: Africans and the Japanese Experience', *Africanews*, 22 February 2017, www.africanews.com/2017/02/22/the-japanese-experience-for-africans-focus.

17 I strongly rely in this section on Anne Allison (2013).

18 See www.un.org/en/development/desa/population/publications/ageing/replacement-migration.shtml.

19 In October 2015, Japan launched an ambitious policy to increase the country's birth rate, calling it a 'national priority'. A new ministry was established and charged with 'building a society in which a hundred million people can be active'. It was aimed at more than simply increasing the birth rate from 1.4 children per woman of child-bearing age (the same as in Germany) to 1.8 (much closer to France's 1.93). Its goal was also to increase the number of women in the job market and increase the employment rate among the rapidly growing number of people who were nearing sixty-five years old.

20 CNN, 17 August 2018, https://edition.cnn.com/2018/08/16/health/life-expectancy-uk-us-drop-study-intl/index.html.

21 In August 2013, the Pew Research Center published a survey on 'Living to 120 and Beyond: Americans' Views on Aging, Medical Advances and Radical Life Extension' to explore the disruptions that century-old lives might create in family structures and inheritances among different generations. See https://assets.pewresearch.org/wp-content/uploads/sites/11/2013/08/Radical-life-extension-full.pdf.

22 This is only an order of magnitude since definitive departures from the United States were only recorded beginning in 1908. But we know that women left less frequently than men, and that the rate of return from America varied greatly according to nationality. The Irish (6 per cent), the Czechs (8 per cent) and the English (10 per cent) returned to their homeland far less frequently than did Hungarians (49 per cent), Croats (60 per cent) and southern Italians (61 per cent).

23 With Charles Piot's kind permission, I borrow this quote, and the one that follows, from his forthcoming book on the US visa lottery.

By Way of Conclusion: Some Plausible Scenarios for the Future

1 The World Bank (2017: 17) underscores 'the fact that Africa is urbanizing while poor – indeed, strikingly poorer than other developing regions with similar urbanization levels'.

2 In the eyes of Hervé Le Bras, a prominent demographer, France is already much of a melting pot, due to a 'generalization of mixed parentage'. In an interview on France Info, on 20 November 2015, he pointed out that '40 per cent of the children born in France had one parent or grandparent of foreign origin'. See http://geo polis.francetvinfo.fr/la-migration-dans-lhistoire-vue-par-le-demog raphe-herve-le-bras-86439.

3 Cf. Vahlefeld 2017; like many commentators during the summer of 2015, the author speculates about the extent to which the warm welcome of migrants in Germany had anything to do with clearing the debts of the Nazi past – *Vergangenheitsbewältigung* – a familiar trope in the German migration debate.

4 Renaud Girard, 'L'immense enjeu des migrations', *Le Figaro*, 4 July 2017.

5 Of course, there were peaks in asylum requests before the wars in Iraq, Afghanistan and Syria, for example in 1992, when ethnic cleansing in the former Republic of Yugoslavia caused an unprecedented exodus and 670,000 people sought refuge in EU countries. But despite the ebb and flow of refugee crises, a clear long-term trend emerges over the past fifty years.

6 Cf. Frédéric Bobin and Jérôme Gautheret, 'Entre Libye et Italie, petits arrangements contre les migrants', *Le Monde*, 15 September 2017; and Jason Horowitz, 'Italy's "Lord of Spies" Takes on a Migration Crisis', *New York Times*, 4 August 2017.

Bibliography

Abani, Chris (2004) *GraceLand*, Farrar, Straus and Giroux.

Ajavi, J. F. Ade (1996) 'L'Afrique au début du XIXe siècle: problèmes et perspectives', in *Histoire Générale de l'Afrique. VI. L'Afrique au XIXe siècle jusque vers les années 1880*, UNESCO.

Akpan, Uwem (2008) *Say You're One of Them*, Abacus.

Alexander, Robin (2017) *Die Getriebenen: Merkel und die Flüchtlingspolitik: Report aus dem Innern der Macht*, Siedler Verlag.

Allison, Anne (2013) *Precarious Japan*, Duke University Press.

Allison, Simon (2014) 'Counting Refugees in Conflict Situations', *Africa in Fact*, No. 21, pp. 5–10.

d'Almeida Topor, Hélène, Coquery-Vidrovitch, Catherine and Goerg, Odile (1992) *Les jeunes en Afrique*, tome 1 (*Évolution et rôle, XIXe et XXe siècles*), tome 2 (*La politique et la ville*), L'Harmattan.

Appadurai, Arjun (2006) *Fear of Small Numbers: An Essay on the Geography of Anger*, Duke University Press.

Argenti, Nicolas (2002) 'Youth as a Resource', in Alex de Waal and Nicolas Argenti (eds), *Young Africa: Realising the Rights of Children and Youth*, Africa Research and Publications.

Ariès, Philippe (1960) *L'Enfant et la vie familiale sous l'Ancien Régime*, Plon.

Baldwin, James (1962) 'Letter from a Region in My Mind', *The New Yorker*, 17 November.

Barth, Fredrik (1969) *Ethnic Groups and Boundaries: The Social Organization of Culture Difference*, Little, Brown and Company.

Bawer, Bruce (2002) 'Tolerating Intolerance: The Challenge of Fundamentalist Islam in Western Europe', *Partisan Review*, Vol. 69, No. 3.

Bawer, Bruce (2006) *While Europe Slept: How Radical Islam is Destroying the West from Within*, Doubleday.

Bayart, Jean-François (1989) *L'État en Afrique. La politique du ventre*, Fayard.

Bayart, Jean-François (2010) 'L'Afrique "Cent ans après les indépendances": vers quel gouvernement politique?', *Politique africaine*, No. 119, pp. 129–57.

Berenson, Edward (2011) *Heroes of Empire: Five Charismatic Men and the Conquest of Africa*, University of California Press.

Betts, Alexander and Collier, Paul (2017) *Refuge: Transforming a Broken Refugee System*, Allen Lane.

Beucher, Benoît (2009) 'La naissance de la communauté nationale burkinabè, ou comment le Voltaïque devint un "Homme intègre"', in *Sociétés politiques comparés. Revue européenne d'analyse des sociétés politiques*, No. 13, pp. 1–107, www.fasopo.org/sites/default/files/article_n13.pdf.

Birg, Herwig (2001) *Die demographische Zeitwende – Der Bevölkerungsrückgang in Deutschland und Europa*, C.H. Beck.

Birg, Herwig (2014) *Die alternde Republik und das Versagen der Politik. Eine demographische Prognose*, Lit Verlag.

Birg, Herwig (2016) 'Die Gretchenfrage der deutschen Demographiepolitik: Erneuerung der Gesellschaft durch Geburten im Inland oder durch Zuwanderung aus dem Ausland?', *Zeitschrift für Staats- und Europawissenschaften (ZSE)*, Vol. 14, No. 3, pp. 351–77.

Bonar, James (1885) *Malthus and His Work*, Macmillan and Co.

Bourguignon, François (2012) *La mondialisation de l'inégalité*, Seuil.

Brunel, Sylvie (2014) *L'Afrique est-elle si bien partie?*, Editions Sciences Humaines.

Carey, Martha (2006) '"Survival is Political": History, Violence, and the Contemporary Power Struggle in Sierra Leone', in Edna G. Bay and

Donald L. Donham (eds), *States of Violence: Politics, Youth, and Memory in Contemporary Africa*, University of Virginia Press, pp. 97–127.

Central Intelligence Agency (2001) *Long-term Global Demographic Trends: Reshaping the Geopolitical Landscape*, www.cia.gov/library/reports/gen eral-reports-1/Demo_Trends_For_Web.pdf.

Césaire, Aimé (1935) 'Négreries. Jeunesse noire et assimilation', *L'Étudiant noir*, March.

Charbit, Yves and Gaimard, Maryse (2015) *La bombe démographique en question*, PUF.

Chasteland, Jean-Claude and Chesnais, Jean-Claude (2006) '1935–2035: un siècle de ruptures démographiques', *Politique étrangère*, No. 4, pp. 1003–16.

Cincotta, Richard (2008) *Half a Chance: Youth Bulges and Transitions to Liberal Democracy*, ECSP Report, No. 13; www.wilsoncenter.org/sites/default/files/ECSPReport13_Cincotta.pdf.

Cincotta, Richard, Engelman, Robert and Anastasion, Daniele (2003) *The Security Demographic: Population and Civil Conflict After the Cold War*, Population Action International.

Collier, Paul (2009) *Wars, Guns, And Votes, Democracy in Dangerous Places*, HarperCollins.

Collier, Paul (2013) *Exodus: How Migration is Changing Our World*, Oxford University Press.

Cooper, Frederick (2002) *Africa since 1940: The Past of the Present*, Cambridge University Press.

Coquery-Vidrovitch, Catherine (1985) *Afrique noire. Permanences et ruptures*, L'Harmattan.

Debusman, Robert (1993) 'Santé et population sous l'effet de la colonisation en Afrique équatoriale', *Matériaux pour l'histoire de notre temps*, Nos. 32–3, pp. 40–6.

Ehrlich, Paul (1968) *The Population Bomb*, Buccaneer Books.

Epstein, Helen (2017) *Another Fine Mess: America, Uganda and the War on Terror*, Columbia Global Reports.

Fanon, Frantz (2004) *The Wretched of the Earth*, trans. Richard Philcox, with commentary by Jean-Paul Sartre and Homi K. Bhabha, Grove Press.

Ferenczi, Imre (1938) 'La population blanche dans les colonies', *Les Annales de Géographie*, Vol. 47, No. 267, pp. 225–36.

Ferguson, James (2006) *Global Shadows: Africa in the Neoliberal World Order*, Duke University Press.

French, Patrick (2008) *The World Is What It Is: The Authorized Biography of V. S. Naipaul*, Picador.

Frontex (2016) *Africa-Frontex Intelligence Community Joint Report 2016*, https://frontex.europa.eu/assets/Publications/Risk_Analysis/AFIC/AFIC_2016.pdf.

Gifford, Paul (1998) *African Christianity: Its Public Role*, C. Hurst and Co.

Godwin, Peter (2006) *When a Crocodile Eats the Sun: A Memoir of Africa*, Little, Brown and Company.

Golaz, Valérie et al. (2012) 'Africa: A Young but Aging Continent', *Population and Societies*, No. 491 (July–August).

Goldstone, Jack, Kaufmann, Eric and Duffy Toft, Monica (eds) (2011) *Political Demography: How Population Changes Are Reshaping International Security and National Politics*, Oxford University Press.

Gubert, Flore (2008) '(In)cohérence des politiques migratoires et de codéveloppement françaises. Illustrations maliennes', *Politique africaine*, No. 109, pp. 42–55.

Gutmann, David (1988) 'Age and Leadership: Cross-Cultural Observations', in Angus McIntyre (ed.), *Aging & Political Leadership*, SUNY, pp. 89–101.

Hardin, Rebecca (2011) 'Concessionary Politics: Property, Patronage, and Political Rivalry in Central African Forest', *Current Anthropology*, Vol. 52, pp. 113–25.

Harding, Jeremy (2000) 'The Uninvited', *London Review of Books*, Vol. 22, No. 3, www.lrb.co.uk/v22/n03/jeremy-harding/the-uninvited.

Harding, Jeremy (2012) *Border Vigils: Keeping Migrants Out of the Rich World*, Verso.

Hart, Keith (1973) 'Informal Income Opportunities and Urban Employment in Ghana', *The Journal of Modern African Studies*, Vol. 11, No. 1, pp. 61–89.

Hatton, Timothy J. (2004) 'Seeking Asylum in Europe', *Economic Policy*, Vol. 19, No. 38, pp. 5–51.

Hatzfeld, Jean (2006) *Machete Season: The Killers in Rwanda Speak*, Picador.

Headrick, Rita (1994) *Colonialism, Health and Illness in French Equatorial Africa*, African Studies Association.

Hertrich, Véronique and Lesclingand, Marie (2013) 'Adolescent Migration in Rural Africa as a Challenge to Gender and International Relationships: Evidence from Mali', *Annals* (July), pp. 175–88.

Hiropoulos, Alexandra (2017) 'Migration and Detention in South Africa: A Review of the Applicability and Impact of the Legislative Framework on Foreign Nationals', Policy Brief 18, African Center for Migration & Society (ACMS), November 2017; http://apcof.org/wp-content/uploads/018-migration-and-detention-in-south-africa-alexandra-hiropoulos.pdf.

Hochschild, Adam (1998) *King Leopold's Ghost: A Story of Greed, Terror, and Heroism in Colonial Africa*, Mariner Books. First French edition: *Les fantômes du roi Léopold. Un holocauste oublié*, Belfond, 1998.

International Crisis Group (2007) *Central African Republic: Anatomy of a Phantom State*, Africa Report 136, www.crisisgroup.org/africa/central-africa/central-african-republic/central-african-republic-anatomy-phantom-state.

International Crisis Group (2015) *The Central Sahel: A Perfect Sandstorm*, Africa Report 227, www.crisisgroup.org/africa/west-africa/niger/central-sahel-perfect-sandstorm.

IMF (International Monetary Fund) (2016) *Sub-Saharan African Migration* (Spillover Notes No. 9).

IOM (International Organization for Migration) (2014) *Fatal Journeys: Tracking Lives Lost During Migration*, www.iom.int/files/live/sites/iom/files/pbn/docs/Fatal-Journeys-Tracking-Lives-Lost-during-Migration-2014.pdf.

IOM (International Organization for Migration) (2018) *World Migration Report 2018*, https://publications.iom.int/system/files/pdf/wmr_2018_en.pdf.

Ismail, Olawale (2009) 'The Dialectics of "Junctions" and "Bases": Youth, "Securo-Commerce" and the Crises of Order in Downtown Lagos', *Security Dialogue*, Vol. 40, Issues 4–5, pp. 463–87.

Jerven, Morten (2013) *Poor Numbers: How We Are Misled by African Development Statistics and What to Do About It*, Cornell University Press.

Jones, Reece (2016) *Violent Borders: Refugees and the Right to Move*, Verso.

Kaplan, Robert (1994) 'The Coming Anarchy: How scarcity, crime, overpopulation, tribalism, and disease are rapidly destroying the social fabric of our planet', *The Atlantic Monthly* (April).

Karl, Kenneth (2000) 'The Informal Sector', *The Courier*, Vol. 178, pp. 53–4.

Kenyatta, Jomo (1979) *Facing Mount Kenya*, Heinemann.

Knight, Franklin W. (1996) 'La diaspora africaine', with contributions from Yusuf Talib and Philip D. Curtin, in *Histoire Générale de l'Afrique, VI. L'Afrique au XIXe siècle jusque vers les années 1880*, UNESCO.

Kohnert, Dirk (2006) *Afrikanische Migranten vor der 'Festung Europa'*, GIGA Focus, No. 12, www.giga-hamburg.de/de/system/files/publica tions/gf_afrika_0612.pdf.

Laqueur, Walter (2007) *The Last Days of Europe: Epitaph for an Old Continent*, Thomas Dunne.

Last, Murray (2005) 'Towards a Political History of Youth in Muslim Northern Nigeria 1750–2000', in Jon Abbink and Ineke van Kessel (eds), *Vanguard or Vandals: Youth, Politics and Conflicts in Africa*, Brill, pp. 37–54.

Leahy, Elisabeth, with Robert Engelman, Carolyn Gibb Vogel, Sarah Haddock and Tod Preston (2007) *The Shape of Things to Come: Why Age Structure Matters to a Safer, More Equitable World*, Population Action International.

Leonardi, Cherry (2007) '"Liberation" or Capture: Youth in between "Hakuma" and "Home" during Civil War and its Aftermath in Southern Sudan', *African Affairs*, Vol. 106, No. 424, pp. 391–412.

McGovern, Mike (2011) *Making War in Côte d'Ivoire*, C. Hurst and Co.

Mahajan, Vijay (2008) *Africa Rising: How 900 Million African Consumers Think*, Prentice Hall.

Malan, Rian (2012) *The Lions Sleep Tonight*, Grove Press.

Manning, Patrick (2010) 'African Population: Projections 1850–1960', www.manning.pitt.edu/pdf/2010.AfricanPopulation.pdf.

Manning, Patrick (2013) 'African Population, 1650–1950: Methods for New Estimates by Region', http://mortenjerven.com/wp-content/uploads/2013/04/AfricanPopulation.Methods.pdf.

Mara, Moussa (2016) *Jeunesse africaine, le grand défi à relever*, Mareuil.

Marshall, Ruth (2009) *Political Spiritualities: The Pentecostal Revolution in Nigeria*, University of Chicago Press.

May, John and Guengant, Jean-Pierre (2014) 'Les défis démographiques des pays sahéliens', *Études*, No. 4206, pp. 19–30.

Mbembé, Achille (2016) *Politiques de l'inimitié*, La Découverte.

Melber, Hennig (2016) *The Rise of Africa's Middle Class: Myths, Realities and Critical Engagement*, Zed Books.

Memmi, Albert (1965) *The Colonizer and the Colonized*, Orion.

Michaïlof, Serge (2015) *L'Africanistan. L'Afrique en crise va-t-elle se retrouver dans nos banlieues?*, Fayard. English edition: *Africanistan: Development or Jihad*, Oxford University Press, 2018.

Millman, Noah (2015) 'The African Century', *politico.com*, 5 May, www. politico.com/magazine/story/2015/05/africa-will-dominate-the-next-century-117611.

Moss, Todd and Majerowicz, Stephanie (2012) 'The Generation Chasm: Do Young Populations Have Elderly Leaders?', Center for Global Development, 3 February, www.cgdev.org/blog/generation-chasm-do-young-populations-have-elderly-leaders.

Mudimbé, Valentin (1988) *The Invention of Africa: Gnosis, Philosophy, and the Order of Knowledge*, James Currey.

Museveni, Yoweri (1997) *Sowing the Mustard Seed: The Struggle for Freedom and Democracy in Uganda*, Macmillan.

Naipaul, V. S. (1983) 'A Prologue to an Autobiography', *Vanity Fair* (April).

Null, Schuyler (2011) 'One in Three People Will Live in Sub-Saharan Africa, Says UN', *The Security Beat*, 8 June 2011; www.newsecuritybeat. org/2011/06/one-in-three-people-will-live-in-sub-saharan-africa-in-2100-says-un.

Ogawa, Naohiro et al. (2008) 'Japan's Unprecedented Aging and Changing International Transfers', talk given at the conference 'The Demographic Transition in the Pacific Rim', Seoul, 19–21 June, http://ntaccounts.org/doc/repository/OMCM%202008.pdf.

Olopade, Dayo (2014) *The Bright Continent: Breaking Rules & Making Change in Modern Africa*, Mariner Books.

Packer, George (1984) *The Village of Waiting*, Farrar, Straus and Giroux.

Packer, George (2006) 'The Megacity: Decoding the Chaos of Lagos', *The New Yorker*, 13 November, www.newyorker.com/magazine/2006/11/13/the-megacity.

Piot, Charles (1999) *Remotely Global: Village Modernity in West Africa*, University of Chicago Press.

Piot, Charles (2010) *Nostalgia for The Future: West Africa After the Cold War*, University of Chicago Press.

Putnam, Robert (2000) *Bowling Alone: The Collapse and Revival of American Community*, Simon & Schuster.

Radelet, Steven (2010) *Emerging Africa: How 17 Countries Are Leading the Way*, Center for Global Development.

Richburg, Keith (1997) *Out of America: A Black Man Confronts Africa*, Basic Books.

Said, Edward (1978) *Orientalism*, Pantheon.

Sander, Thomas and Putnam, Robert (2010) 'Still Bowling Alone? The Post-9/11 Split', *Journal of Democracy*, Vol. 21, No. 1, pp. 9–16.

Sauvy, Alfred (1946) 'Évaluation des besoins de l'immigration française', reprinted in *Population*, Vol. 71, No. 1 (2016), pp. 15–22.

Schmitz, Jean (2008) 'Migrants ouest-africains vers l'Europe: historicité et espaces moraux', *Politique africaine*, No. 109, pp. 5–15.

Severino, Jean-Michel and Ray, Olivier (2010) *Le Temps de l'Afrique*, Odile Jacob. English edition: *Africa's Moment*, trans. David Fernbach, Polity, 2011.

Sommers, Marc (2006) *Youth and Conflict: A Brief Review of Available Literature*, www.crin.org/en/docs/edu_youth_conflict.pdf.

Sommers, Marc (2015) *The Outcast Majority: War, Development, and Youth in Africa*, University of Georgia Press.

Smith, Stephen (2015) 'The Elite's Road to Riches in a Poor Country', in Tatiana Carayannis and Louisa Lombard (eds), *Making Sense of the Central African Republic*, Zed Books, pp. 102–22.

Spinks, Charlotte (2002) 'Pentecostal Christianity and Young Africans', in Alex de Waal and Nicolas Argenti (eds), *Young Africa: Realising the Rights of Children and Youth*, Africa Research and Publications.

Sullivan, Rachel (2003) *Managing Modernity: African Responses to Rapid Population Growth*, Doctoral thesis at the University of California, Berkeley.

Tabutin, Dominique (2007) 'Les relations entre pauvreté et fécondité dans les pays du Sud et en Afrique subsaharienne. Bilan et explications', in Benoît Ferry (ed.), *L'Afrique face à ses défis démographiques. Un avenir incertain*, Karthala, pp. 253–85.

Taub, Ben (2017) 'The Desperate Journey of a Trafficked Girl', *The New Yorker*, 10 April, www.newyorker.com/magazine/2017/04/10/the-desperate-journey-of-a-trafficked-girl.

Taylor, Paul (2014) *The Next America: Boomers, Millennials, and the Looming Generational Showdown*, Public Affairs.

Tilly, Charles (2007) *Democracy*, Cambridge University Press.

Tribalat, Michèle (2013) *Assimilation, la fin du modèle français*, L'Artilleur.

United Nations Population Division (1999) *The World at Six Billion*, www.un.org/esa/population/publications/sixbillion/sixbillion.htm.

United Nations Population Division (2000) *Replacement Migration: Is It a Solution to Declining and Ageing Populations?*, www.un.org/esa/population/publications/migration/migration.htm#.

United Nations Population Division (2015) *World Population Prospects. The 2015 Revision*, www.un.org/en/development/desa/publications/world-population-prospects-2015-revision.html.

United Nations (2017) *International Migration Report*, www.un.org/en/development/desa/population/migration/publications/migrationreport/docs/MigrationReport2017_Highlights.pdf.

Vahlefeld, Markus (2017) *Mal eben kurz die Welt retten: Die Deutschen zwischen Größenwahd und Selbstverleugnung*, epubli.

Vellut, Jean-Luc (1996) 'Le bassin du Congo et l'Angola', in *Histoire Générale de l'Afrique. VI. L'Afrique au XIXᵉ siècle jusque vers les années 1880*, UNESCO.

Vennetier, Pierre (1976) *Les villes d'Afrique tropicale*, Masson.

Wellman, Christopher Heath and Cole, Phillip (2011) *Debating the Ethics of Immigration: Is There a Right to Exclude?*, Oxford University Press.

World Bank (2017) *Africa's Cities: Opening Doors to the World*, report authored by Somik Vinay Lall, J. Vernon Henderson and Anthony J. Venables, https://openknowledge.worldbank.org/handle/10986/25896.